Rural Roots

Photographs by Hugh Robertson

Rural Roots

Pre-Confederation Buildings of the York Region of Ontario

Mary Byers, Jan Kennedy, Margaret McBurney,
and The Junior League of Toronto

UNIVERSITY OF TORONTO PRESS Toronto and Buffalo

© University of Toronto Press 1976
Toronto and Buffalo
Printed in Canada

Library of Congress Cataloging in Publication Data

Byers, Mary.

Rural roots.
Bibliography: p.
Includes index.
1. Historic buildings – Ontario – York (Regional Municipality) 2. York, Ont. (Regional Municipality) – History. I. Kennedy, Jan, joint author. II. McBurney, Margaret, joint author. III. Robertson, Hugh. IV. Title.
F1059.Y6B9   971.3′54   76-26867
ISBN 0-8020-2230-8
ISBN 0-8020-6287-3 pbk.

THE JUNIOR LEAGUE OF TORONTO

As an important and enduring part of the celebration of its 50th anniversary in 1976, the Junior League of Toronto provided the funds which made possible the extensive photography required for this volume. As a result, the publisher was able to secure the services of Mr Hugh Robertson of Panda Associates to photograph more than 150 buildings scattered over the 663 square miles of what is now the Regional Municipality (formerly County) of York.

The inventory of historic buildings in York County, which led to this book, was initiated in 1966 with support from the Government of Ontario and under the direction of the late Professor W.S. Goulding. The Junior League volunteers involved in that research are too numerous to mention individually. Their time, enthusiastically given, produced the inventory of York County pre-Confederation structures now in the Ontario Archives - a part of the inventory of the province which may serve as an instrument in preserving the best of our architectural heritage.

was heated by eight fireplaces, only one of which remains today. The white picket fence was also moved from the Yonge Street site. Dr Langstaff had copied it from an 1812 picket fence in Sharon.

'Drynoch Farm,' Lot 60, Concession 1E, on the Jefferson Sideroad, was built about 1845 by Captain Martin Donald McLeod - 'a gentleman of the highest standing and respectability,' who came from the Isle of Skye. His impressive home, set in lovely grounds, stood on 600 acres of land. It has been altered considerably over the years but the central portion dates from 1845. Like many settlers of means from the British Isles, Captain McLeod tried to reproduce the atmosphere of his homeland and therefore surrounded his home with fine landscaping and filled it with furniture, china, and paintings which he had brought with him.

One of McLeod's nine children, Col. James Alexander Farquharson McLeod, served with the North West Mounted Police when the force first entered the West; Fort McLeod was named after him. As

Front door, 'Holmwood'

the guidebook, *Explore Richmond Hill*, notes, 'His work in the West paved the way for the construction of the C.P.R., the first practical link binding the nation together. His strength and diplomacy prevented the Canadian West from following the pattern of lawlessness set farther south.'

The Oak Ridges–Lake Wilcox area, north of Richmond Hill, was the site of an early experiment in settlement of which nothing remains, but which was a striking example of poor judgement in high places. To escape the French Revolution, thousands of French noblemen had made their way to England for refuge. This influx was expensive for the British government to sustain and some relief was sought. Comte Joseph Geneviève de Puisaye headed one group of these Royalists. He was in good favour with the British Prime Minister, William Pitt, who together with William Windham, Secretary of War, devised a plan of settling French emigrants in Upper Canada. This scheme had the support of government officials at

'Drynoch Farm,' Jefferson Sideroad

York, but their motives were questionable, for they thought that this settlement would provide a buffer against possible attacks by Indians from the north. The settlement was ill planned and therefore doomed to fail; most of the noble inhabitants succumbed not to the tomahawks of the Indians but to the rigours of pioneer life. The marquises, counts, viscounts, and their ladies arrived in the wilds of York County in 1800. Comte de Puisaye called the settlement Windham after the Secretary for War, but soon lost the vision of a future community and left for Niagara, returning finally to England in 1802. On the restoration of the monarchy in France, most of the émigrés went back to their homeland. The vast scheme, which was to have given de Puisaye a settlement of 5,000 acres of land stretching up to Lake Simcoe, had collapsed; yet, while they were here, the group added a colourful note to wilderness life. Occasionally the ladies were able to be present at social functions in York, where their jewels caused a considerable sensation. Of the

'Crosby Hall,' 38 Bedford Park Avenue

original group, only 13 families were still at Windham in 1802 and, within ten years, most of these had departed.

One who remained was Laurent Quetton St George, who became a merchandizer on a grand scale. He had six depots on the Great Lakes and a store in York at King and Frederick Streets, which was the first building built of brick in the town of York. 'Glen Lonely' at Wilcox Lake was a three-storey French château, the home of St George's son Henri. Banquet halls and wine vaults served to entertain York's important families. Henri lived at 'Glen Lonely' in the midst of luxury until his death in 1897.

Chevalier Augustus Bointin, another French nobleman, once owned the property on which 'Crosby Hall' is located (38 Bedford Park Avenue). The house was built by Parker Crosby about 1863, on a 100-acre farm. It exhibits a variety of architectural styles and features a central cupola.

'Hove-to,' 4 Elizabeth Street North, is of uncertain date but may

'Hove-To,' 4 Elizabeth Street North

have been built as early as 1830. Its asymmetrical facade suggests a
date closer to 1850, however. The upper windows contain the original glass panes. Farley Mowat, the author, lived in this house as a
child and it is thought that his grandfather gave the house its name.

An interesting house of which little is known is located at 63
Major Mackenzie Drive. There is evidence to indicate that the property was part of the holdings of Benedict Arnold, who, as noted in
the chapter on Georgina, had been granted many thousands of acres
by the British crown for services rendered. In all probability this
house was a farmhouse built about 1850. It was once owned by
Ada Mackenzie, a well-known golf champion. During her ownership, it was restored from a dilapidated condition to its present
attractive state.

Of historic interest is a modest cottage at 525 Carrville Road,
south of Richmond Hill. Of board-on-board construction and covered by stucco, it is one of the oldest houses in Richmond Hill. The

63 Major Mackenzie Drive

front door is bolted by its original lock and opened by a four-inch key. The house recently has been acquired by the Richmond Hill Historical Society, which is restoring it. The Society believes that Rowland Burr built this house and brought his bride here in 1819, when he was renting the property, and ran a mill which he owned on the stream. During the initial stages of restoration, a stencilled wall was uncovered under layers of paper and plaster. Such stencilling was a common and inexpensive way to decorate walls, often done by itinerant painters, and fashionable during the period between 1800 and 1840.

4

Aurora

From 1827, when the first sawmill was built, until the railroad arrived, Aurora was a small milling town. In 1851, Machell's Corners, as it was then called, had an estimated population of about one hundred, probably less - a quiet, insignificant village compared with neighbouring Thornhill with its bustling activity; on the streets of Thornhill, twice that number of farmers would be lined up on a Saturday to use one of the town's several mills. Yet according to the census of 1881, the population of Aurora had jumped by that time to 1540; the reason for this growth being the railroad. The railroad which by-passed Thornhill and further weakened its already failing industry ran directly through Aurora and brought it prosperity. From the day in 1853 when Upper Canada's first steam locomotive, the 'Toronto,' made the journey north on the new Ontario, Simcoe, and Huron Railway, the boom began in Machell's Corners. Aurora became for a time the 'Head of Rail,' and coal and lumber yards were as well filled as the freight sheds.

Until this time, Yonge Street in Aurora had been sparsely settled, and therefore few early buildings remain. The boom in house building came chiefly in the 1850s, when industry and settlers were moving into the railroad town. The original Yonge Street ran parallel to the Yonge Street which bisects Aurora today, and only traces are left of it. It had been built to by-pass the valley on the main route, which became a bog in the spring and fall. Road improvements required for motor traffic eventually eliminated this problem and the by-pass was no longer necessary. The former by-pass is now known as Old Yonge Street.

The oldest house in Aurora, and one of the earliest in York County, is located at 41 Yonge Street North. Built in 1795, it is believed to have been the hunting lodge of an American. Since this was barely one year after Augustus Jones first blazed Yonge Street, it shows remarkable enterprise for a hunting cabin to be constructed in such a remote wilderness. To York from the eastern United States, plus the hazardous trip north from there through bush country, would have been an arduous journey for even the most eager sportsman. It may be that the unknown hunter who built the house in 1795 was a member of the surveying team commissioned by Governor Simcoe to survey Yonge Street.

The house must have been built of logs as no other materials would have been feasible then. It is now covered with stucco. The style is 'Cape Cod salt-box,' which is rare in Ontario, but common in the eastern United States.

This home was later bought by a Quaker, Charles Doan (or Doane),

41 Yonge Street North

who lived there before he moved across the street. Doan, shoemaker and merchant, was later reeve of the village and postmaster of the township. It was he who changed the name from Machell's Corners to Aurora. In the mid-19th century, he moved from the 'salt-box' to an elegant provincial town house across the road. This house was a casualty of time and development, and it no longer stands at the town centre.

The 'Manor House' at 72 Yonge Street North has been described as one of the finest examples of Gothic revival in the province. It was built about 1855 by Dr Walter Geikie, a prominent physician, who was Dean of a medical school in Toronto that later joined the Faculty of Medicine of the University of Toronto. The porch, with its elaborately carved cathedral-like arches, is a remarkable example of the Gothic influence. Its peaked gable is embellished by a generous application of 'gingerbread,' which follows the roof line. Eventually, such mouldings were mass produced but, in earlier

'The Manor House,' 72 Yonge Street North

homes such as this, the carving was done by the hand of the owner or builder.

The two rooms at the front of the Geikie house were used as the consulting room and the dispensary. A back wing was added by the Hillary family in 1870, which contains a ballroom on the upper level with a finely decorated ceiling. The brickwork of the exterior is of good quality and as much thought was given to its intricate pattern as to the carved 'gingerbread.' Patterned brick, an attempt to copy the columned lines of classical architecture, was a source of pride in the 19th century, unique to southern Ontario. This house was designated as an historic site in 1975 by the National Historic Sites and Monuments Board because of its unique architecture. The Board provided the funds for the building of the new fence, a replica of the original.

At 14 Mosley Street is the church now occupied by the Salvation Army. It was built by the New Connexion Methodists, and it is

Gothic revival: Dr Walter Geikie's 'Manor House'

thought that it was designed by John Howard, the Toronto architect. It is similar in design to three other of Howard's churches, the Presbyterian Church in Willowdale, St John's York Mills, and the Anglican Church in Holland Landing. It was built of red brick made in a local brickyard but has been painted white. Since the construction date is probably 1856, it is the only church in Aurora which has been standing for over one hundred years.

Wellington Street was one of the earliest streets to be settled after the railroad brought industry and rapid settlement to Aurora. At 17 Wellington Street, the Henry Machell house (the first name of Aurora, Machell's Corners, was derived from this pioneer merchant), is a lovely Georgian-type house built in the 1850s. The two-storey style is common in Aurora and several such houses, like Machell's, have stucco over the original frame. The Ardill store at Wellington and Yonge was the original Machell hotel and livery.

Farther along Wellington Street, No. 38 is similar in style to the

38 Wellington Street, built by Edward Andrews

Machell house, but without the shutters and the imposing door. The frame construction has not, however, been stuccoed over and the house has been maintained beautifully. It was built by Edward Andrews in the middle of the 19th century as a home and as a shop for his tailoring business. It is an interesting building because although it is small the proportions are grand - a miniature of the larger Georgian homes. The house next door is almost identical, probably it had the same builder.

The home at 58 Wellington Street, of a similar style, dates from 1861. The front door is enclosed by a semi-circular portico supported by pillars. Originally the main floor windows were french doors opening onto a verandah. The verandah was later removed and replaced by the present portico.

On Wellington Street East there are reminders of Aurora's position in the 1850s as 'Head of Rail.' The old Railroad Hotel, built about 1850, is located at the station where it served the first travel-

The 'Red House,' Yonge Street north of Aurora

lers by steam locomotive. Alternative accommodation could be found in the same area at a second hotel, which had the delightful name of 'The Pig's Ear.' Imagination is needed today to visualize this section of Aurora as it was in those busy days.

The 'Red House,' a fine brick home on Lot 85, Concession 1, just north of Aurora, was built by Thomas Cosford Sr, a blacksmith and carriage-maker. One of the earliest houses on Yonge Street (1828-30), it is set well back from the highway and the original Old Yonge Street runs immediately behind the house. The house stayed in the Cosford family until 1928 when it was purchased by George Leacock, brother of the famous humorist. It is still referred to as the Leacock house by many local residents.

The front of the house has three sets of french windows, the middle one hung off-centre. The present owner believes that this window was once a door, as there is evidence of an early fan transom and a doorsill remains. These, and other structural details, suggest

'Willow Farms,' Yonge Street north of Aurora

that the house was built as a Regency cottage. (Built mainly in the 1830s and 1840s, a Regency cottage was a small, square house, usually surrounded by a verandah. The roof had a shallow pitch, and often French doors led from the house to the verandah.)

Across the road from the Red House is 'Willow Farms,' which was built by Thomas Cosford for his son Thomas Jr, who was born in the Red House. Although the porch has been altered and dormers added, its beautiful Georgian simplicity remains undisturbed. Two other early buildings stand on the land: a brick carriage house and a gardener's cottage. The property has been exceptionally well maintained through the years. The surrounding area was long known as Cosford's Corners.

Just south of Aurora, in the grounds of the North York Hunt Club, is an Ontario Gothic house given to the Hunt Club by Lady Eaton. The simple verandah has been altered slightly but otherwise the style is typically Gothic with the centred gable and double

Gardener's cottage, 'Willow Farms'

chimneys. The rounded window under the gable and the curved side windows date the house in the post-1860 period.

William Trent, an early business associate of Robert Simpson of Newmarket, founder of the department store, located his home, 'Ballymore Farm,' on Lot 86, Concession 1E. The back portion was built in 1835 and the front in 1840. The brick has been painted, but the original form of the building has been preserved so well that it is still an extremely attractive home. In the kitchen the original brick fireplace with pine mantel remains.

'Ballymore Farm'

5

Newmarket

Newmarket is situated in a key geographical location. It is near the junction of four rivers - the Humber, the Don, the Holland, and the Rouge. These rivers have provided transportation ever since the Indians used them as fur-trade routes, for they gave easy access from Lake Ontario to Georgian Bay and beyond. They were known as branches of the Toronto Carrying Place.

The settlement of Newmarket is tied, as are all settlements on Yonge Street, to the decision made by John Graves Simcoe to have a trail blazed along the course of the Don River by Augustus Jones in 1794. Governor Simcoe's decision was based upon the ease of portage on the Don Trail as compared with the Humber. The origin of the name Newmarket is self-evident: the village was a market close to Lake Simcoe which could handle purchase or exchange of products, saving the customer the long trip down to the town of York. In the early 1800s several mills and stores were built in Newmarket by the first settlers. By 1814 there were two frame and several log buildings in the village as well as the nearby mills.

The first name in the settlement of the Newmarket area is Timothy Rogers. A United Empire Loyalist and a Quaker, he came to the Newmarket area in 1801 in search of lands for forty Quaker families who wished to leave the revolutionary violence in the eastern United States. It is believed that he was the first white man to spend the night on the site of Newmarket. Rogers was so pleased with this location for the Quaker families that he secured a grant immediately for forty 200-acre farms. He himself received Lots 92,

93, 94 and 95 on the west side of Yonge Street just south of High-way 9. In 1809, he was on the move again, leading another party of settlers to Pickering Township, but his family remained in the Newmarket area and built houses there.

When Timothy's group first arrived, they were given two years to clear and fence 10 acres of their land and build a house 16 by 20 feet of logs or frame with a shingled roof. Like all settlers on Yonge Street, they had to clear 35 feet in front of their property, half of which was to be public road (Yonge Street). In addition to the Rogers family, the Quaker settlement included Samuel Lundy and Isaac Phillips. Near by were Charles Doan, Watson Playter, Henry Widdifield, and others.

Since most of this sizeable band of settlers in the Newmarket area belonged to the Society of Friends, the Yonge Street Friends were granted a Preparative Meeting in 1804 by the Philadelphia Yearly meeting. The Friends first met at settlers' homes, but in 1807 Asa Rogers gave the land for a cemetery, and in 1810 William Doan gave the two acres directly north of the cemetery for a meeting house. The Meeting House which was erected on Lot 92, Conces-sion 1W, Yonge Street, still stands as it was built in 1810. The quiet hour of meditation is still observed in this meeting hall. Over the years it has been virtually unaltered. Its simple board-and-batten construction was so sound that, with the exception of re-roofing and minor alterations to the porch, no changes were made for 165 years. A restoration program was finally undertaken in 1974-75. The building is divided down the centre with a sliding partition, and separate exits are provided for men and women. This was the earliest building constructed for religious purposes north of the town of York. The stones in the burying ground to the south bear many old settlers' names. A descendant of James Starr, an early Quaker set-tler, explains that Quakers were buried in order of the date of their deaths, so family names are scattered. Sometimes family pride had to be swallowed, therefore, when a beloved relative was interred beside an 'undesirable' Friend.

On Lot 92, Concession 1W, immediately south of the Quaker Meeting House, is a home built in 1818 on the old Timothy Rogers grant of land. It is of frame and stucco construction, and retains its original door and verandah. The bay window is a later addition.

In the town of Newmarket there are other Rogers houses. The large house at 457 D'Arcy Street was built in the 1830s of local brick. It is a substantial two-storey building of excellent proportions. The door is surrounded by the early glass panes. Beneath the peaked gable is a high-columned portico; this is a later addition. A smaller Rogers house built in the 1830s is next door at 451 D'Arcy Street. (The name of the street is in memory of D'Arcy Boulton who came to Upper Canada from England in 1805 and became solicitor-general, attorney-general, and judge; 'The Grange,' connected with the Art Gallery of Ontario, was once his home. The family name of Boulton has been long associated with Newmarket.) Another Rogers house is at 602 Pearson Street. It was built in the late 1820s, and is similar to the D'Arcy Street house, also of red local brick, but without the elaborate additions and shutters.

One of the most important Quakers to accompany Timothy Rogers was Isaac Phillips who was instrumental in building another Quaker meeting house. Phillips became established on Lot 89, Concession 1W, in 1806, and the two-storey building which stands today on Yonge Street is built around his 1808 house. It is set well back on the west side of Yonge, just across from Fairmead School. The 1808 portion may have replaced an earlier temporary log house, for Isaac Phillips was residing on his property in 1806 and was already a member of the school board for the first Quaker school. The present front portion of the house is a later addition, built of 3-inch thick clapboard and now covered with stucco, but at the side of the house the early part of the building can still be found. The peaked gable indicates the 1808 section now embodied in the later structure. The property is now known as 'Armking Farms.'

Newmarket's history has included many prominent and distinguished families, well known throughout York County and beyond. One of the most prominent was that of the Robinsons. Christopher Robinson was a United Empire Loyalist, son of the President of the Province of Virginia. He moved first to the Maritime Provinces and later to Upper Canada, where he was a member of the Assembly from 1796 to 1798. His widow, Esther, married Elisha Beman in 1802, uniting her family with that of the rugged pioneer from New York State who had settled in Newmarket in 1795. Esther's five children grew to make noteworthy contributions in public service. One son, Peter, was, as noted, founder of Peterborough and owner of the Red Mill in Holland Landing. Another son, Sir John Beverley Robinson, was Chief Justice of Upper Canada. A third, W.B. Robinson, was a colonel in the militia and held many public offices in Newmarket.

Elisha Beman had vast energy and imagination. He envisioned mills, ferries, and shops in the northern section of Yonge Street to serve fur traders and travellers, but it was not until 1806 that he was able to turn his ideas into reality. He built a mill and purchased Joseph Hill's mill and stores and also was responsible for building a distillery and an ashery. The 'ashery' may need explanation. Ontario pioneers collected wood ashes and boiled them in water until lye crystals formed, which could be used in making soap. Sometimes the lye was made on the farmer's own property, using a large iron kettle for the boiling. An 'ashery' served the same purpose in the early community on a larger scale.

The Beman-Robinson house (the oldest in the town of Newmarket) was built in 1825 by Joseph Hill and was moved in 1855 from Lot 93 to its present site at 448-450 Eagle Street. When Elisha and Esther lived in the house it was still situated on Lot 93, where it was a centre for social activity in the area. Among those who stopped at the house were Dr John Strachan, first Bishop of Toronto, Lieutenant-Governor Maitland and Lord Dalhousie, Governor-in-Chief of British North America, Sir John Franklin, the famous explorer, and many other political, military, and religious leaders. The house is a simple one-and-a-half storey dwelling originally built in wood which subsequently has been covered with stucco. Its chief interest is its early date and the history connected with it.

John Bogart arrived in Upper Canada from Pennsylvania in 1802 following a scouting trip by Martin Bogart in 1789. The four years between Bogart's first trip and his eventual move to Upper Canada were spent in disposing of all his assets in Pennsylvania which were not portable. After making the journey to York with their belongings, including animals, and trees and seeds for a future garden, the Bogarts made the further journey up Yonge Street and finally settled at what was later Bogarttown (see chapter on Whitchurch).

In less than ten years, Bogart had made a successful business and built a good permanent home. John Bogart later moved into the town of Newmarket and died in his house at the corner of Prospect and Gorham (253 Prospect Street).

The Bogart house at 897 Mulock Drive was built for Philip Bogart, son of John Bogart, in 1849. The house is constructed of red brick available locally at this date and its imposing size and quality indicate the prosperity of the family.

Another of Newmarket's successful millers was Eli Gorham, who arrived in the Newmarket area in 1808 with four carding machines for the manufacture of woollen goods. It is possible that these were the first to operate in York County. From 1811 Gorham ran mills and a factory on various sites until, in 1836, he put up his last building and worked it until his death, supplying a wide market with woollen products.

In addition to his manufacturing, Eli Gorham was a successful farmer. He built a brick house in Newmarket in 1836 at 674 Gorham Street. Today the brick has been painted and a frame addition covers the door. The house is built in the Georgian style which was so popular with those whose success enabled them to build the kind of large permanent home they wanted. There are interesting elliptical windows on the side of the house. This was undoubtedly Eli's second or third home, as he had been in Newmarket since 1808 and had probably built a log or frame dwelling on this property first.

Timothy Millard house, 445 Botsford Street

Timothy Millard had come from Pennsylvania to establish a mill in York County in the year 1805. He settled first in Stouffville and did not reach the Newmarket area until 1812. There, he and his father purchased 200 acres of land and began farming, building a red frame house which stood until 1878 when it collapsed into the nearby stream. Timothy, having brought his stones from the Pennsylvania mill, was anxious to put them to use. The Millards were the fourth family of millers in Newmarket and Timothy and his son John located their gristmill on what became Mill Street. In 1834 Timothy built the house at 445 Botsford Street. Later Timothy Street was named for him. As with the other millers, this home postdated his first more humble dwelling. Later additions have been made: the door and window panes have been changed and the brick painted.

Stephen Howard house, Yonge Street

John Millard, Timothy's son, built a house which stands on Yonge Street at the Holland Landing turn-off. The stucco building was completed in the 1830s and has the elliptical windows under the eaves frequently seen in Newmarket.

On the west side of Yonge Street, Lot 102, Concession 1W, is the Stephen Howard house. It is south of the John Millard home and the Holland Landing turn-off. Howard was a Quaker who came from Vermont in 1801. This house, built in 1849 for his son Stephen, is situated impressively at the end of a long tree-lined driveway. It is a beautiful example of simple Ontario Gothic style.

Stephen Jr subsequently traded this Yonge Street farm for 100 acres of property on Green Lane, east of Yonge Street, Lot 101, Concession 1E. The red brick house which stands on the property today, unchanged, was built in 1849. Its centre hall plan was the most common to be found in the country but individuality always was possible and is demonstrated here in the barge-board on the peaked gable. The early glass remains in the windows and the farm bell which announced meals to the workers in the fields in the 1850s is still in use, mounted on the back shed which is of the same date as the house.

Botsford Street holds two examples of historic and architectural interest. In the 1830s a prosperous local merchant, James B. Caldwell, built the house at 438 Botsford. Caldwell stood with the rebels in 1837, and feelings ran high in Newmarket, as elsewhere, between rebel sympathizers and Family Compact supporters. Local legend holds that Caldwell and his wife provided food for the military prisoners of the Rebellion of 1837 who were being held in the Old Kirk on Timothy Street behind the house. He also acted as a go-between for the prisoners and their families. There were at one time 46 prisoners in the Old Kirk who had been arrested when William Lyon Mackenzie's lists of sympathizers were found after his flight. The house was called 'Liberty Hall,' a further indication of James Caldwell's political views. James owned a chair and paint factory in the Caldwell Block on Main Street. Previously he had rented a house and shop on Mill Street from Mordecai Millard. His Botsford Street house is stucco over brick with a small side addition. Small windows under the eaves (this time square), and a porch are variations of the basic Georgian style. An interesting feature of the interior is an original portrait of a dog painted on the wall at floor level for the children of the family. The dog appears to emerge from a hole in the wall. A 400-year-old white oak tree stands in the yard behind the house.

One of Newmarket's favourite sons was Robert Simpson, and although his home at 384 Botsford Street, built in 1866, dates slightly later than our period of interest, its importance in the community necessitates mention. Curved windows replaced the simple early type as the 19th century progressed and here they indicate the later date of this house. Robert Simpson was a Scottish immigrant who came to Canada at the age of 22 and settled in Newmarket. In 1858 Robert opened his first store in partnership with William Trent as 'Simpson and Trent, Groceries, Boots, Shoes and Dry Goods.' The store was at Main and Timothy Streets. Later he became the partner of M.W. Bogart and, finally, in 1871, moved to Toronto to open the store at Queen and Yonge Streets which became the large department store chain and mail-order house. Simpson's wife was

'Liberty Hall,' 438 Botsford Street, built by James B. Caldwell

Mary Ann Botsford, the daughter of a successful Newmarket harness-maker.

The inhabitants of Newmarket had a keen interest in education and were anxious to provide a school where the classical languages and literature could be taught. The grammar school at the corner of Raglan and Millard Streets (139 Raglan Street) was built in the 1840s and here Sir William Mulock was first educated. The Common School Act of 1816 had provided funds for the payment of teachers which were to be divided among communities according to population. But even earlier, in 1806, the Quakers had begun teaching when the monthly meeting was granted and from 1823 there had been common (public) schools in Newmarket. The grammar (private) school at Millard and Raglan charged fees of £4, £3, and £2 per term. The school is now a private dwelling of white stucco and the windows have been altered.

While William Mulock was attending the Newmarket Grammar

Robert Simpson's home, 384 Botsford Street

School, he lived in the house at 567 Pearson Street built in the 1840s by John Dickson, principal of the Newmarket Grammar School. The Mulock family came to Newmarket after the death of William's father because Mary-Cawthra Mulock had family ties there, and she purchased the Pearson Street home to raise her family in it. The Rt Hon. William Mulock was subsequently Postmaster General of Canada, Minister of Labour, and Chief Justice of the Supreme Court of Ontario. The Mulock estate on Yonge Street, one mile south of Newmarket, is an imposing family home. It is set back from the road as are all the major early estates, it being as desirable to ensure privacy in the mid-19th century as it is today. The back portion of the Mulock house is the earliest; it is a sizeable brick structure and its original windows are intact. The front section is of a much later date but blends with and augments the early section, with its imposing gables, pillars, and porch.

The Cawthra and Mulock names are influential throughout New-

Mulock residence, 520 Yonge Street

market's history, although the Cawthra association is older. John and William Cawthra were sons of a wealthy Etobicoke pioneer, Joseph Cawthra, who settled in Newmarket around 1820. At that time the Cawthras owned most of Pearson Street and a business on Main Street. The John Cawthra home is on the north side of Water Street at the corner of Main. It was here that Mary Mulock was born. John Cawthra opened a general store and a distillery. He was a successful merchant and, in addition, was a hard-working public servant. The Cawthras were not on the side of the Family Compact and therefore not in official favour, so when John fought in the War of 1812, he served in the ranks as a private. John knew Samuel Lount and John's son Henry recalled in later years his father's impassioned pleas to Lount to avoid involvement with the rebels.

The red brick house at Water and Main replaced John Cawthra's frame house built on the site in 1820. In 1865 it was the location

'Dawson Manor,' Yonge Street

Front door, 'Dawson Manor'

of the first bank in Newmarket, of which John Cawthra was manager. It now houses apartments and a store.

The King George Hotel on the west side of Main Street was welcoming travellers in 1845. It was the custom of the coaches then to stop frequently to refresh horses and passengers at the inns. Eventually, the King George (which has been called successively the Railroad Hotel, Forsyth House, Pepher House, and Proctor House) became a temperance hotel. The old King George Hotel is much altered today but beneath the signs and additions is the simple brick structure of the 1840s.

Dawson Manor off Yonge Street, on Lot 2, Concession 1W, was built in 1830 and has been lived in by the Dawson family since that time. It is located on the west side of Yonge Street just past the first set of lights north of Highway 9. When Squire Dawson came from Yorkshire, England, on a chartered sailing vessel, he brought with him all the household and farming necessities he felt he would require in Upper Canada. He brought materials to build a house, workers for his farm, housebuilders, and servant girls for the home. Unfortunately, the sailing vessel was blown off course and landed south of New York city. Dawson, his wife, four sons, the labourers, servant girls, livestock, and building materials proceeded in a caravan up to York and from there north to Newmarket. Upon their arrival, Squire Dawson was able at last to put his vast supplies to use and build his permanent home. The brick house features two large french doors flanking the imposing fan-transomed central door which is enclosed by ornate brickwork. The unusual brickwork and design of the house indicate that the workmen and materials were not local. Although many of the wealthy pioneers like Squire Dawson brought quantities of furnishings from the Old Country, they seldom imported actual building materials and the retinue that Dawson did. In the interior, the hand-blown glass Squire Dawson used for the windows is still in good condition. All the wood trim was hand-carved and the baseboard in every room is carved differently.

Another early name connected with Newmarket is that of Jacob Aemilius Irving. Irving was born in Charleston, South Carolina, and the influence of the southern plantation style can be seen in the Irving house on Lot 3, Concession 1W, off Yonge Street just north of Dawson Manor. Jacob Irving purchased the property from Theodore Huntley in 1839 for $6,048. Huntley insisted that the whole amount be paid in silver pieces, so the Bank of Upper Canada counted out 6,048 silver pieces to Huntley at the close of the transaction. Local hand-made bricks and stone from the property were used in the construction in 1841 of Irving's house, which was called 'Bonshaw,' after the Irving ancestral home in Dumfries, Scotland. Among Irving's friends were many members of the Family Compact, including the Robinson family. Jacob Irving was appointed first warden of the district of Simcoe and in 1843 was called to the Legislative Council. Often he was seen in his four-in-hand carriage 'issuing from the gates of Bonshaw and whirling along Yonge Street into town.'

'Bonshaw,' Yonge Street

6

Holland Landing

During the middle of the 19th century, Holland Landing was a bustling and thriving community. Early residents recalled traffic jams along the main street: 'at times it was difficult to cross the street, there was such a stream of ox carts and wagons coming from the river at the end of the street. They brought logs to the saw mill, tan bark to the tanneries and wheat to the flour mills. Farmers' wagons with the grain and livestock added to the congestion' (*The History of County of York, 1885*). All of this is difficult to imagine today, for now little remains to remind us of the village's past importance. The railway which caused a building boom in Newmarket in the 1850s and 1860s signalled the decline of growth in Holland Landing.

Holland Landing was named after Major Samuel Holland, first surveyor-general of Canada. Its location on the Holland River leading out of Lake Simcoe made it an important stopping-place in travel between Lake Simcoe and Lake Ontario. Long before East Gwillimbury was settled, the trail used by Indians on their way to the Great Lakes led through Holland Landing. Settlers arrived in the area after Yonge Street was improved, and by 1825 a stagecoach was operating daily between Holland Landing and the town of York.

Prominent in the early history of the town was Peter Robinson, for whom, as noted, the city of Peterborough was named. Peter Robinson purchased the first gristmill in Holland Landing and in 1821 built the Red Mills. These large mills were well known throughout York County and their flour was shipped to many parts of Europe as well as to other areas of Upper Canada. By 1831, a steamboat, the *Peter Robinson*, was transporting settlers from Holland Landing across Lake Simcoe to the town of Barrie, and providing pleasure tours. Peter Robinson became commissioner of crown lands in 1827, but resigned in 1836, because of disagreement with Sir Francis Bond Head. He died in 1838.

North of Holland Landing, on the west side of Dalhousie Street north of Doane Street, is a white frame house which Peter Robinson built near the Red Mills on Lot 111 in the 1820s. A simple verandah surrounds the building on three sides. This house was rented to Francis Phelps, who used it as a tavern, but it continued to be referred to as the 'Robinson Inn.'

Another house occupied by Peter Robinson is located by the railroad where Yonge Street and the tracks meet. The house can be recognized from Yonge Street by the early twelve-paned windows

Peter Robinson house, Dalhousie Street

which are visible from a distance. These windows are typical of the high-quality workmanship throughout the house. All the interior woodwork is walnut, and the basement contains the original pegged beams. The basement fireplace shows evidence of the pot-arm which was used in cooking. Every room in the house had its own fireplace. A sturdy stone foundation supports the house and the name of the builder and first owner is cut in stone above the back door, 'W.J. Sloane 1836.'

Another well-known resident of Holland Landing during the 19th century was Samuel Lount. He and his brother George were sons of Gabriel Lount of Bristol, England. Gabriel settled first in Pennsylvania, but preferring to live under British rule, he and his Quaker wife came to York County in 1811. Samuel became a blacksmith, married, and moved to Holland Landing. He was the representative for the Simcoe area in the House of Assembly from 1834 to 1836.

Peter Robinson house, Yonge Street

When Sir Francis Bond Head became lieutenant-governor, Reformers such as Lount, Mackenzie, and Peter Mathews were hopeful he would support reforms, giving more power to the elected Assembly, but were disappointed. In the 1836 election, most Reformers were defeated, including Lount, and they alleged much corruption in the election practices of their opponents. Samuel Lount eventually played a major role in the Rebellion. When it failed, he attempted to escape to the United States, but was captured, tried for treason, and hanged along with Mathews.

Many of the reforms for which Samuel Lount fought were later granted, and a plaque in his memory has been erected in Holland Landing. The blacksmith shop no longer exists where Lount manufactured pikes as weapons for the Rebellion when he was not drilling with the rebels or attending rebel rallies. It is reported that Lount practiced shooting at a hollow loaf of bread, buttered, since Sir

Christ Church, Holland Landing

Francis Bond Head had said that the discontented settlers would not rebel because 'they know too well which side their bread is buttered on.'

The first post office in Holland Landing was owned by Lount's brother George and this house is still standing on Main Street across from the Anglican Church. The original brick has been painted green.

A few other buildings in Holland Landing are of architectural and historical interest. Two early churches are still in use: the Methodist (United) Church at School Street and Peter Street, built in 1842, and Christ Church (Anglican), built in 1843. The latter building is particularly attractive and is in excellent repair. It stands on top of a small hill, surrounded by the cemetery and overlooking the town's main street. The plan of the church, built according to a design by John Howard, is similar to St John's York Mills.

The Blackstone house at 16 North Street is of interest because it

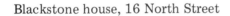

Blackstone house, 16 North Street

was the home of the first lawyer in the area, Henry Blackstone. Although a clever and talented man, his downfall was brought about by 'demon rum' and he died in 1852 after being brutally beaten in a tavern brawl. Today his home bears a sign saying 'Gospel Centre,' and is used as a nursing home for the aged. It is a simply designed but attractive house. The unique doorway has a brick arch sitting directly on wooden Doric columns. The bricks, made locally, vary in colour from salmon to deep red: they are small in size and laid in Flemish bond. This method alternates headers and stretchers (a stretcher is the side face of the brick and a header the end).

At one time there were four hotels in Holland Landing, in which, on occasion, the village residents danced to music supplied by local talent. The McClure Hotel is a two-storey building with Georgian features. This old hotel has now been restored and its brick painted green. Also recently restored is the 1850 house at 442 Yonge Street.

McClure Hotel, Bradford Street

Originally red brick, it has now been painted white and new shutters set off the symmetrical windows (the old twelve-paned windows have been replaced).

A handful of other houses which were built during the middle of the last century still stand today in Holland Landing, but little else remains of what was once a thriving community. The town did, however, attain a measure of fame towards the latter part of the 19th century because of the large frogs which were harvested from the Holland River. For several years frogs' legs were shipped from the town to New York and other large cities for the enjoyment of epicures. The business ran into trouble, however, with the arrival of carp in the river; the carp fed on the frogs and soon a novel and profitable industry came to an end.

442 Yonge Street

7

Markham Township

William Berczy was chiefly responsible for the orderly and permanent settlement of Markham Township as well as parts of Vaughan, Whitchurch, King, East Gwillimbury, and York. It was to Markham Township that Berczy led a group of approximately sixty-four families in 1794. These people, most of whom were from Hamburg, Germany, had been lured by agents of the British government with offers to locate on a settlement at Poultney, New York. They had expected, when coming to the new world, to own their own land, but found on their arrival in the Genesee area that they would be employed as tenant farmers, working the land for its owners.

For a year these families suffered extreme hardships and injustice. They were accused of conspiracy for not participating in a cooperative farm arrangement and were actually chained and jailed, allegedly for reneging on this deal. When Berczy's settlers were starving, placards were nailed on local inns and tavern walls warning the local population against giving credit to him. The settlers were followed everywhere they went by the landowners' agents and threatened when they complained about their treatment. Berczy himself was accused of being 'insolent, drunken and idle,' and sued for money that he had spent on his two hundred 'worthless' individuals. Finally, Berczy learned of Lieutenant-Governor Simcoe's offer of free land grants to settlers who were willing to locate in Upper Canada, and was thus able to rescue his people.

In 1794 his small group journeyed north on foot and settled primarily along the banks of the Rouge River in Markham Township. En route they were forced to stay in the town of York for approximately a year, during which time Berczy finalized the arrangements for grants of 64,000 acres. Berczy used this year to inspect, survey, and plan for future development of this land tract. While exploring the possibilities of mills on the Rouge River, Berczy discovered that with the removal of a considerable amount of debris, travel inland by boat was feasible from the mouth of the Rouge on Lake Ontario to within twenty miles of the Holland River. Berczy felt that if he could divert the Yonge Street trail through Markham Township, the extra commerce it would provide would benefit his whole settlement.

Berczy therefore made a proposal to Simcoe that he would have his settlers homestead the river lots. Each settler would be responsible for clearing his share of the river in order to make it navigable. Berczy himself would design and build a canal from the headwaters of the Rouge River to the Holland River; in return, Simcoe was to grant Berczy land at and around the mouth of the Rouge River in order that he might build warehouses, wharves, and a good harbour. Simcoe agreed to this plan and thus the lots along the Rouge River were the first to be settled in Markham Township.

Berczy's dream of a canal and the increased trade and commerce it would bring never materialized. Lieutenant-Governor Simcoe instead accepted a gift of £12,000 from the North West Company to improve the old trade route, Yonge Street, which was in deplorable condition. Simcoe used some of this money to patch the worst parts of the road and spent the rest buying up all of the land at the mouth of the Rouge River which he had promised to Berczy. By the time Berczy had settled his people and was ready to implement his plan, he found that the land on which he had counted was no longer available.

For any settlement to succeed at that time, access to building materials and food was imperative. When Berczy's settlement finally started, he was advised by Simcoe to build the first saw and grist mill in Markham Township in what was later to be called German Mills (Lot 4, Concession 3, on the Don River). Philip Eckardt, one of the settlers, had brought with him from Pennsylvania all the necessary equipment to start both a saw and a grist mill. The German Mills consequently had a pair of French burrs and complete machinery for making super-fine flour. A great deal of the grain ground in these mills came from the United States by schooner to be made into flour in Canada, because the product of this superior Canadian milling enjoyed preferential treatment on the English market.

Word of the 'good mills and thriving settlement of Germans' reached the United States and, little by little, more settlers began to arrive from Pennsylvania, New York, Virginia, and New Jersey. These people came to Canada not only to obtain free land but also to escape from the extreme religious persecution to which they had been subjected by Puritan America. For these reasons settlements of Mennonites, Quakers, Lutherans, and Tunkers were established throughout York County.

Philip Eckardt was outstanding among the settlers. He was the only one of the group, apart from Berczy, who had any education. He had joined Berczy in New York State because he had fallen in love with a young girl, Ann Elizabeth Koepke, a member of the original group. Eckardt proved invaluable to the settlers as he was a millwright, land surveyor, skilled mechanic, and carpenter; in addition, he had previously owned and built mills in Pennsylvania and New York. He was a large man, six feet, six inches of inexhaustible drive and energy. In addition to operating the German Mills he assisted in the survey of Markham Township in 1794 - the first township survey completed in Upper Canada. He was foreman in the erection of government buildings, including the Parliament Buildings in the town of York. His efforts were rewarded: for building and equipping the German mills he received a 200-acre lot direct from the crown, and for operating the mills for ten years, £2,000. His name, which appears as 'Philip Eckardt' in his will, has been spelled 'Eckhardt' by some of his descendants and by historians.

William Berczy was a talented and highly educated man, an idealist and a dreamer. Without these qualities, and his determination to find good land and conditions, he would never have succeeded in bringing settlers to Markham Township. But, as previously noted, he was beset with problems from the time of the initial landing in Pennsylvania. Obviously, in view of the financial troubles which followed him continually, he could not have been a practical business man. Eckardt, on the other hand, was enough of a realist to make a financial success of all his endeavours. Personality differences led to a clash between the two men and, after ten years, Eckardt moved away and settled at what is now Unionville, taking with him some of the original Berczy group. A number of houses, still occupied today, were built there by these settlers.

Philip Eckardt's original log house, built for him in 1794, still stands on Lot 17, Concession 6, north of Unionville. It has been altered completely, however, and now the only feature identifying it as a typical Pennsylvania-German building is the wide overhanging eaves, which protected the log walls from the effects of rain and snow, and sheltered people entering or leaving the house. The house is built of squared white pine timbers, 32 inches across, with all the corners dove-tailed. Originally it had an upper and lower verandah and three full storeys. The lower storey has been removed so that the present house is only two storeys high.

The original interior layout of the house is interesting because it indicates the typical way of life of the German settler. On the ground floor there was a large dining-room and two bedrooms, one for the head of the family and his wife and the other for the minister, who had to live with his parishioners, changing his residence from time to time. The kitchen usually was an adjoining room under a separate roof. The second floor was one large room occupied by all the girls of the family and the third floor was a large single room for the boys.

Being a devout Lutheran, Eckardt held church meetings in his house until 1819, when he gave a grant of land for the establishment of St Phillip's Lutheran Church and cemetery. This log church was replaced by a frame and later a brick structure in 1862, and was then moved to its present location in Unionville. The Lutheran church is no longer known as St Phillip's. It was changed to Bethesda to avoid confusion with St Phillip's Anglican, which was originally built across the road from the Lutheran church.

The Eckardts had eighteen children. Seven of their sons grew to manhood and farmed along Kennedy Road south of their father's lot. Their houses provide examples of nearly every type of building material and architectural style of that period. On the west side of the main street, in what is now referred to as the 'old town,' stands the original home of Dr Thomas Eckardt, architecturally the oldest in Unionville. It was built around 1820 of mud brick and faced with stucco which now has been painted a deep red, and is one of the few mud brick dwellings still standing in the township. It is occupied by Mr E.J. Stiver, a descendant of one of the original settlers.

In the 1800s, this mud brick construction was fairly popular. The main reasons for the use of mud or adobe brick were that it was cheap and that its production required nothing but a bed of suitable

On the original Eckardt house,
the wide eaves remain

Philip Eckardt's original log house, altered by later tenants

clay and unskilled labour. An oval pit was dug and filled with clay and water. After twenty-four hours or more, when the clay was properly wet, oxen were brought to tread on it. During the trampling, short straw was thrown in – four bushels of straw to one hundred bricks. Then the mud was poured into moulds, 6 × 12 × 18 inches, and left until the bricks were dry enough to be taken out and stood on end. When thoroughly dry, they were stacked up to 'season' under some kind of protection from the rain. These mud bricks were laid using a mortar composed of equal parts of pure clay and sand. Usually the exterior walls were covered with stucco and, as in German log or timber houses, a thirty-inch overhang or verandah around the entire house protected the stucco from the elements.

Across the street from the home of Thomas Eckardt is the Salem Eckardt house. Until recently, it was owned and occupied by a descendant of Philip Eckardt's. A board-and-batten house, it has

Thomas Eckardt house, 206 Main Street, Unionville

decorated gables and is built on a stone foundation. The bark-covered pine beams which support the house are laid transversely (a feature of German barn design) and, after nearly one hundred and fifty years, show little or no evidence of wood deterioration. Locally referred to as 'barn built,' this method of building was used so that at any time the house could be lifted from its foundation and moved to another location without structural weakening. For several years the Salem Eckardt house was the home of Frederick Varley, the artist and member of the Group of Seven.

Another son, Gottleib Eckardt, owned considerable property on the north-east corner of Kennedy Road and Highway 7, but his house is no longer standing. Gottleib was one of the town's more controversial and colourful characters. He was an ardent follower of William Lyon Mackenzie during the Rebellion, which did not endear him to many of the residents of Unionville, most of whom supported the Family Compact. Gottleib incurred the displeasure

Salem Eckardt house, Main Street, Unionville

Salem Eckardt house

of the official party and was convicted of high treason and sentenced to death. He had organized some of the horseback relays used by Mackenzie and his followers to carry coded messages to their supporters sprinkled throughout the County of York many miles from each other. These dispatches were picked up by a rider from a messenger at one point and taken to another messenger some distance away. In order not to be caught and charged with treason, the riders pretended to be making routine trips through their local areas. Gottleib's sentence eventually was changed to banishment to Van Diemen's Land and later, with the help of a Markham magistrate, he was granted a full pardon. His fight for reform had incurred such enmity, however, that on his death in 1856, his family, fearing that his grave would be molested, had his coffin buried very deeply and four-inch white oak planks, 40 feet long and running in various directions, embedded in the soil over the top of his coffin.

The house now standing on Gottleib's original property was built by his son William in 1852. It was the first house in Unionville constructed of regular brick from the Snowball brickyard in Markham Township. (This unusual name for a brickyard was derived from that of its owner, John Snowball.) William's home is an exceptionally handsome Gothic style house, beautifully proportioned, with french doors flanking an elegant main entrance. The brick has now been painted white; it is evident that the present owners take pride in preserving this early home and have adapted it successfully for modern living.

The Eckardt family clearly played a major part in the establishment and development of Unionville. In the middle 1800s the Toronto-Nipissing Railway was built through Unionville and the town started to develop around the railroad station, which was slightly to the north of Gottleib's farms. By this time the Eckardt family and the families of other original settlers had increased in numbers to such an extent that small sections of Eckardt's original farm were sold for the construction of individual family dwellings. The Lutheran church bought some of the property and moved the church building down to the section of the farm where it stands to this day.

Unionville remains a fine example of the past blending with the present. Few rural communities in the county of York have as many original buildings, both residential and commercial, which are still in use and still in excellent condition. Along the main street of

Front door,
William Eckardt house

William Eckardt house, 124 Main Street, Unionville

Unionville, north of Highway 7, may be seen the Lutheran manse at 109 Main Street; it was built in 1867. An original settler's house, which once served as a bank, is located at 133 Main Street. The planing mill built in 1835 is still in use. The jail, now a residence, is at 145 Main Street on a small branch of the main road. The blacksmith's shop, the hotel (beside the fire hall), and the post office (194 Main Street) remain from the early period. The side streets of the old town also yield examples of typical early Ontario architecture and on the outskirts of the town can be seen many homesteads of original settlers. One of the best can be found on Lot 15, Concession 5, on the south side of 17th Avenue. It was built of stone in 1852 by Francis Stiver, a son of one of the original Berczy group. In a recent addition, the owner has built behind it another fieldstone house, similar to the original and connected by a one-storey passageway. The result is a splendid example of building for today while adding to the beauty of yesterday. The quality of materials

133 Main Street, Unionville, once a bank

and workmanship used in the addition is outstanding. Both new and old stones show lovely colours, and it is remarkable how closely matched are the new stones to those used over a hundred years ago.

The name of Reesor is well known in Markham Township. The origins of this prolific family can be traced back to Berne, Switzerland, where Peter Reesor was born in 1713. Although he himself emigrated to Philadelphia, dying in Lancaster County in 1804, he fathered one of Markham's oldest and most influential clans. A Zurich Bible dating from the 1570s accompanied him from Berne and was brought to Markham in 1804 in a Conestoga wagon by the family. This remarkable book bearing Peter's signature is a family treasure to this day.

Peter's son Christian was responsible for the move from Philadelphia to Upper Canada. He first sent his son Peter, one of ten children, to scout the land. Peter was directed from York to the Rouge River. He was enthusiastic about the good land and water

145 Main Street, the former Unionville jail

he found there, and when, on the return journey, he met an ex-
officer of the British army who offered him a remarkable trade -
400 acres of land for Peter's horse, saddle, and bridle! - he accepted
it. He returned to Pennsylvania on foot carrying the halter, which
had not been part of the deal. This halter is now kept in Markham
Township by the family, who cherish it. Such a transaction was not
as unusual as it may seem, for the Mennonites were renowned for
their skill in breeding and training horses, and in Upper Canada land
was cheap while good horses were rare.

Peter, his father Christian, his brother Christian, and his other
brothers and sisters came north to their land and located on Lot 14,
Concession 10, in 1804. Unfortunately, the elder Christian was
killed by a falling tree while clearing the woods two years later. A
stone cairn was erected to his memory by the family at the north-
east corner of Highway 7 and the 10th line.

The original Reesor homestead no longer exists, but on the site

Unionville's former blacksmith shop, Main Street

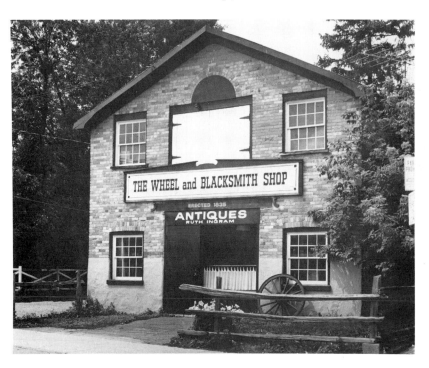

of the first settlement on Lot 14, Concession 10, is located a house built in 1840 by Christian, grandson of the first Christian. The barns are as old as the house and there is a small family cemetery at the rear. The property runs down to the river, where once there was a dam and a sawmill. From 1939 until 1955, this house was also a cheese factory. Another Reesor home, built by the same man, one which is still in the family, lies south on Lot 12, Concession 9. Christian, who built it, married Elizabeth Cornell of the family that founded Cornell University. They had six children. Later, a widower aged 74, he married her 19-year-old niece and raised another five children. The family names, as well as the properties, have been handed down through the generations, and the owner of the house in 1976 was Lloyd Christian Reesor. This stone farmhouse, dating from 1849, was called the 'Old Home Farm.' This designation can be seen faintly etched on the north doorway. The fieldstone used in many Mennonite houses such as this was often collected over a period of years before the house was begun. The stones were selected carefully for their colouring, and sometimes also for their association with a particular event of their discovery - perhaps a damaged implement, or a minor accident!

Another Reesor home, on Lot 1, Concession 10, has stayed in this family since it was built by John Eby Reesor in 1853. This house has passed through the hands of John, Benjamin, Abe, Henry, and Willis Reesor. A small house at the rear is the original settler's cabin, but it has been sheeted over with tin. The barns remain as they were built, and the land is still farmed.

A beautiful white brick Reesor home built in 1853 by Abraham, son of Christian, is just south of Markham village on Lot 8, Concession 8. Beautifully proportioned, it has a delicate Gothic window above the door. Today the private home of an antique dealer, it is now called 'Canadian Homesteads.'

Just on the county line, Lot 1, Concession 11, stands the old Reesor church. The first church, which was built of logs in 1820, was shared by Presbyterians and Mennonites - an early ecumenical movement fostered by necessity. During the week it was a school and on Sundays a church. The language used in this school of 1820 might well have been German: in this township containing so many German-speaking settlers from the Berczy or Pennsylvania-Dutch groups, German would have been a common language and a speaking knowledge of it probably necessary for anyone engaged in trade.

Another prominent early settler was George Miller, a native of Dumfriesshire, Scotland, who emigrated in 1832 and located in 1837 on Lot 16, Concession 9, with his wife Catherine. He imported Leicester and Cotswold breeds of sheep and raised them on his farm, 'Rigfoot,' named after a country estate in Scotland. He also imported Shorthorn-Durham cattle. All of the animals, and even the trees he planted on the property, were brought from Scotland. George Miller was instrumental in establishing the Provincial Exhibition, a forerunner of the Canadian National Exhibition at Toronto, and was active in it for the rest of his life. His brick home, built in 1837, has the thick walls typical of its period, and the planks inside the house are all original, as are the L-shaped barns, which have never been painted.

One of the first families to settle east of Concession 6 was that of John Marr. Marr was a colonel in the British army who arrived

'Canadian Homesteads,' built by Abraham Reesor, south of Markham

in Markham in 1801 and, with a government grant of 600 acres, settled on Lots 12, 13, and 14, Concession 9. His descendants have the original crown deed to his land, dated 1821. The former colonel had to carry his wheat on his back 14 miles to German Mills to be ground, and is noted for having once walked to Toronto to obtain special bread and tea for his family for Christmas. The house his son Ben occupied on this property, Lot 14, Concession 9, was built in 1845. Its old bell tower is still intact. At first the kitchen and pantry were on the first floor and the living-room was upstairs. The porch is as solid as when it was built over one hundred and thirty years ago.

A home belonging to the Button family, known as 'St Clair Farms,' is on Lot 11, Concession 10, at Locust Hill. Built in 1865 for Colonel William Button of the Buttonville family to replace an earlier frame dwelling, it cost £900, including a bonus to the workers if they finished it before Christmas. The bell on the adjacent shed was the community firebell, and the carriage and wood sheds also still stand. The wide carved staircase in the interior is an example of the skill of pioneer carpenters.

The little village of Cedar Grove on Highway 47 southeast of Markham village is typical of a number of early communities that are now represented by only a few remaining buildings. In their day, these were thriving centres and their names still have meaning for older Markham residents who recall Locust Hill, Cashel, Cedar Grove, Mongolia, Sparta, Altona, Milneville, Brown's Corners, Almira, Headford, Mount Joy, and Melville. Although it is difficult now to find these places on a map, they recall the past. In Cedar Grove, Peter Lapp ran a cider mill in 1872, which was operated entirely by machinery powered by horses. It is still a cider mill, but it now uses electricity. The Cedar Grove schoolhouse of 1869 is now a Markham Township Community Centre. Cedar Grove's blacksmith shop, built about 1860, still stands on Lot 3, Concession 10.

Another military man who settled in Markham Township was Captain William Armstrong of the British army and the York Rangers, who was born in England in 1792, and emigrated to Upper Canada. He married Esther Reesor, one of Peter's daughters, and lived to be 87. His contribution to the community was notable. He founded the Anglican Church in Markham and gave the land for the rectory, built the Wellington Hotel in Markham village (torn down in 1909), and owned Armstrong's Whiskey Distillery. He donated the land for the Markham Fair, beginning this annual successful event. His house, built in 1840, is on Lot 10, Concession 8. A stucco building that stands behind the main house was originally erected as quarters for farm help. In 1923 gates were erected to commemorate the 100th anniversary of Armstrong's acquisition of the land.

The village of Markham was described in Smith's *Canada* in the year 1851 as 'a considerable village, containing between eight and nine hundred inhabitants, pleasantly situated on the Rouge River. It contains 2 gristmills, with three run of stones each, a woolen factory, oatmeal mill, barley mill, and distillery, foundry, 2 tanneries, brewery etc. - 4 churches: - Episcopal, Presbyterian, Congregational and Wesleyan.' The village was thus a rapidly growing community which at one time is reported to have supported easily four taverns; it was considered to be a hard-drinking pioneer town.

The first crown grant in the village was to the McIntyre family in 1804, and consisted of Lot 11, Concession 8. This property passed to Joseph Reesor in 1805 who gave the settlement the name of his family, calling it Reesorville. He renamed it Manheim (in the Mennonite dialect 'a man's home') at the request of the other settlers, and finally, again at their request, called it Markham after the township which bore the name of an Archbishop of York in England - William Markham. This name had been given to the township by Lieutenant-Governor John Graves Simcoe. By 1828, a post office had been opened at Markham and mail came three times a week from York.

Most of the early village has disappeared and what remains today represents, with a few exceptions, Markham of the 1860s and 1870s. In this period, Markham boasted three wagon-makers, Speight, Pringle, and Wales. The homes of two of these important members of the community, Speight and Wales, are still located in the village.

James Speight was elected first reeve of Markham village in 1873. His home at 48 Main Street dates from 1870 and the early Speight Wagon Works which he operated stood on the same lot. The house, of the board-and-batten construction so common in Markham, is notable for the barge-board on the eaves. The wagon works had been started in 1840 and, by 1877, when James was operating the business, he owned, along with the wagon factory, a planing mill and a sash and door shop, all of which produced a total annual turnover of nearly $150,000. The goods were exported to the northwest and other parts of Canada. In addition, Speight had a large local trade. Unfortunately, the house has deteriorated, and may easily be disregarded by the passerby.

The other wagon-maker, H.R. Wales, was also a carriage-builder. His 1845 house at 159 Main Street is of yellow brick with black shutters. It has graceful proportions and an elegant verandah. In the rear is an early brick bake-oven which at one time was to be part of the Black Creek Pioneer Village collection. The current owner, a decorator, has also restored an 1850 double house at 63-65 Main Street, taking care to duplicate details – even to the buttermilk paint originally used. This house, named 'Woodfield,' has a tradition of mortgage-free ownerships. The present owner, who never likes to have a mortgage herself, was intrigued to discover that the previous owner and the original builder had felt the same way.

Although the Pringle Wagon Works no longer exist, at one time the three brothers engaged in the business, James, Robert, and

159 Main Street, Markham, built by H.R. Wales

93 Markham Township

159 Main Street

George, manufactured all kinds of sleighs, cutters, wagons, and buggies, employing fifteen men, and deriving a gross income of about $10,000 a year.

These early wagon-makers exhibited their products yearly at the Markham Fair which, even in the 1840s, was an annual event which included a fine horse show. In the very early days the fair is said to have been held alternately at Markham and Unionville. That it was a notable horse show is evidenced by the record that at one spring show 26 aged stallions were exhibited. Among the earlier exhibitors were the Pringle Wagon Works, Wales, Speight, and James Ley (ploughs).

At 14 Ramona Boulevard, Markham, is located the Robinson family home. The property was obtained by crown grant in 1810, and the permanent dwelling on it was erected in the 1840s for a cost of $1,000. This large home housed two generations of Robinsons. James Robinson followed the same trade as his father and

'Woodfield,' 63-65 Main Street, Markham

grandfather, who were tanners, and was reeve of the township from 1868 to 1872.

One of the few American-born immigrants to the township, Ambrose Noble, came before the War of 1812 and settled on Lot 16, Concession 8, in 1816. The distinctive building now on the property was built in 1853 and called 'Ambrose House.' It has clean uncluttered lines and, at one time, was landscaped with great skill and care. Now the road has been widened and comes to the front door, eliminating the attractive planting.

The present home of an antique dealer, on Lot 15, Concession 7, was built in the 1830s by Jacob Wismer. Its construction was board-on-board. It requires no lathing: stucco is applied directly to the boards. In the 1860s, siding was used on the exterior to cover the stucco. The front door still has the original hand-forged lock.

In 1860 the exceptionally fine frame house on Lot 16, Concession 6, was built for Frederick Eckhardt by Henry Wismer on 200

Robinson home, 14 Ramona Boulevard, Markham

acres of land granted to Eckhardt in 1837. The unusual double posts on the verandah have attracted many artists and students of architecture, who also admire the tree-studded setting and the simple lines of the well-preserved board-and-batten building.

Three stone houses attest to the fine skill of the builders, ex-convicts who learned their trade as stonemasons while serving terms in the Kingston Penitentiary after the Mackenzie Rebellion. One of these houses was built about 1860 for Christian Hoover on Lot 29, Concession 7. It is located well back from the road in order to be near a stream. The original log house and bake-oven no longer exist but a smoke-house remains behind the house.

The fieldstone house on Lot 30, Concession 7, which belonged to the Moore family in the 1840s, also owes its initial craftsmanship to the skill learned in the penitentiary, but a new lease on life to its present occupants. The restoration happily blends an addition and modernization with the old building. Old materials were utilized wherever possible to bring about this excellent result.

The third of the stone houses, on Lot 26, Concession 8, belonged to Jacob Birkey. The headstone in the eaves records the date, A.D. 1862, but this was the second dwelling to stand on this property. The family had lived here for fifty years when this second home was built. They probably were descendants of Abraham Barkey or Burkey – as noted earlier, the spelling of family names was variable at this period, and this diversity has led to some confusion.

The brick house on the Gormley-Stouffville road, Lot 35, Concession 7, was built by Henry Bartholomew in 1841. His daughter Catherine married Newbury Button, the son of Francis Button of Buttonville, and the young couple took over her father's home. The bricks for the house were made on the property and the front features a fanlight in the attic and a cobblestone porch.

Two houses of the Hoover family can be seen near the Gormley-Stouffville Road. On Lot 34, Concession 6, stands a house built by Christian Hoover (father of the Christian Hoover who located on Lot 29, Concession 7). It was built in 1865 and is in exceptionally fine condition. An outstanding feature is the fireplace at the rear of the house, in the former kitchen area. Bake-ovens at the side of a fireplace were common and often projected outside the wall, as they were deeper than the fireplace. This one was unusual since it was fired from the outside.

Until recently, Christian Hoover's settler's cabin stood beside this

The old Moore house

Fieldstone house, Lot 30, Concession 7

house. The cabin can be seen today at the Markham Museum. It was a settler's obligation to construct a 'good and sufficient dwelling house' in order to obtain a crown grant, but this cabin shows more than the minimum requirements. The simplest form of settler's cabin had just one room. The Hoover cabin, however, contained two other rooms partitioned off from the main living room-kitchen area. These rooms would have been unheated as the only heat for the dwelling came from the large main fireplace, whose ample proportions enabled it to serve the kitchen, which was the centre of family life and social activity. The attic served as an extra sleeping loft; often it had to be reached by ladder. Hoover's cabin had a porch, a feature which was to become common in early York County, developing into the verandah which often surrounded three sides of a house.

Hoover's cabin in the Museum and the house on Lot 34 demonstrate the sequence in which a pioneer established his homestead:

Henry Bartholomew house, Gormley-Stouffville Road

first he built the initial settler's cabin (in Hoover's case more than the minimum required by the terms of the crown grant); and then after years of work he was able to build the larger permanent dwelling.

Also to the credit of the important Hoover family is a fine field-stone house in Stouffville built in 1852 and located on Lot 34, Concession 9. It looked out on 104 acres of good Markham farm land. The years have only improved the stone of which the house is built. An addition to this home illustrates the way in which the building plan often was dictated by necessity. Whereas in the winter months the main fireplace conveniently served for both cooking and heating, in the summer its heat was unwelcome. The solution was to move the cooking to another area in summer, and hence 'summer kitchens' were built, with space for wood storage.

The name of Stouffville came from the Stouffer family whose lineage is traced from Abraham Stouffer. In 1804 Stouffer walked

Christian Hoover house

all the way from Pennsylvania and took possession of 600 acres of land, a portion of which is now the town of Stouffville. One old Stouffer house exists but the original design has been changed through extensive alterations. Of interest only because of its early date is a brick house at 356 Main Street East. In 1846 the building was a tavern owned by Daniel and Hiram Yake.

The Berczy settlers who came to Markham in the 1790s were, as noted, mainly responsible for the early development of the township, but they were not the first white men to come to the area. Markham had been Indian territory and was purchased from the natives in 1787, at a price which now seems woefully inadequate. The first persons to obtain deeds to land were Thomas Kinnear, John Lyons, and Nicholas Miller. Miller arrived in Upper Canada in 1793. Letters reveal that Mrs Miller referred to herself as the first white woman to live on Yonge Street, and that she began housekeeping in a wigwam. While later settlers usually had neighbours to give them friendly assistance in house building, especially in raising the roof, the Millers could call on no one. They had, therefore, to use timbers that the husband and wife, unassisted, could lift. Fortunately, an unexpected visit from Lieutenant-Governor Simcoe and company, who were returning from a journey to Lake Simcoe, provided the manpower to raise the Miller roof in exchange for a meal.

The Berczy settlers located initially in the south-west corner of Markham Township, and it was not until 1801, when James Mustard arrived from Scotland, that settlement began in the north and east. Mustard was the first white man to settle in the north-central area. James and his brother George located in 1801 on Lot 29, Concession 5. James had come to Markham by way of Pennsylvania, having left Scotland in 1794. George left Scotland shortly after his brother, intending to join him immediately, but his ship was stopped in mid-Atlantic by a British warship and all able-bodied young men were removed and pressed into the marines to serve in the Napoleonic Wars. Several years later George jumped ship while in port in the West Indies, returned to America, and followed his brother into the wilds of Markham. His circuitous trip from Scotland had taken six years. However, he was not totally averse to the king's service; during the War of 1812, while serving as a lieutenant, he was wounded at the western battery during the battle of York and taken prisoner by the Americans. Subsequently he was exchanged and served in the army until the end of the war. Such persistence seems typical of the pioneer spirit. A simple fieldstone house, built in 1862 by one of the family descendants, William Mustard, stands on the original property. Although the interior is much altered, the exterior remains as it was.

Because of their isolation the Mustard brothers considered relocating, but their loneliness was relieved when Henry Wideman arrived from Pennsylvania in 1803 and settled a few miles to the east. He was the first of many Mennonites who made their homes in the township and was the first Mennonite preacher in Markham. He was followed in 1804 by the Reesors, Hoovers, Stickleys, Sherks, Stouffers, and other Mennonite and Tunker settlers. This stream of immigration continued until the war of 1812, by which time there were approximately 1200 residents in Markham - over twice as many as in the town of York. These settlers were all industrious farmers and soon acquired title to their land.

The home of Henry Wideman's son Adam still stands on Lot 33, Concession 4. It was built of brick in 1837; the wood used in its construction, including the verandah which originally enclosed the building, came from one immense pine log brought from Whitchurch Township.

South of the Gormley-Stouffville road lies Bruce's Mill Conservation Area, where the Metropolitan Toronto and Region Conservation Authority has contributed to the preservation of Markham's industrial past by restoring to working order the old mill. An earlier mill was built on the site in 1829 by Casper Sherk, one of the first German settlers. Fourteen years later the property passed to the Bruce family which erected the present mill in 1858. An elevator belt installed at that time is still in operation. The substantial mill house stands near by; its appearance would indicate that it was built in the 1850s.

The Tunkers who settled in Markham Township came from Pennsylvania as did the Mennonites, but differed from the latter on various points of religion. Since they were pacifists by long tradition, Governor Simcoe exempted them from military service. Among the Tunkers the Heise family was prominent. Three Heise brothers came together from Pennsylvania in 1804 and settled in and around Gormley and Victoria Square. A land grant for Lot 33, Concession 3, was given them at this time. The interesting two-storey building on this lot, constructed by Christian Heise and still owned by the

Heise family, has a frame exterior beneath which is the original log structure built in 1830 or earlier. The thick front door made of wide vertical pine boards is reinforced inside with slanted pine boards studded with nails in a pattern of three-inch squares. This door, according to the present generation of Heises, formed a protection for their families against Indians who might attack them from 'up the lake.' The windows have been replaced, the original ones having been small with bars nailed across them for added safety.

The village of Gormley still bears the name of James Gormley, who came to Canada from England at the turn of the 18th century and established a general store and post office in the village. A Gormley home on Lot 31, Concession 4, remains almost unchanged. Near by, on Lot 30, Concession 4, is Richard Lewis's house. Lewis himself was killed while blasting stone for the foundation of his house, and it was purchased shortly thereafter by William Francey, a blacksmith, noted in Gormley for his great skill. The original

Bruce's Mill, in the Bruce's Mill Conservation Area

hewn-timber barn which stood behind Lewis's house was dismantled in 1976 and moved piece by piece to the site of the old Riverdale zoo in Toronto. It will be the first building in an historical domestic farm.

The Gormley and Lewis houses located on the 4th Concession typify the settlement pattern of the township. The population was denser on alternate concession lines, 4th, 6th, 8th, 10th, because the first pioneers built their cabins for companionship on opposite sides of the trail which ultimately became a road. Each built as close to his neighbour across the trail as he could, although location near the water supply on the property had to be the prime consideration in selecting the building site. With this concentration of dwellings for the sake of companionship, the ends of the farms which lay along the next concession lines remained long untouched by the axe. These public roadways continued to be bush trails until the neglected ends of the farms were occupied by the second generation. This growth pattern is evident today as the township's older houses still are to be found mainly on alternate concession lines.

On 18th Avenue, west of Victoria Square, is a Jacob Heise house built about 1840 of solid brick. This is a doddy house, one which contained a section for the retired parents - 'doddy' is a contraction of 'grossdoddy' (grandfather). Mennonites and Tunkers frequently built this type of house so that when the youngest son finally took over operation of the family farm his parents could live at the other end of the house. The older sons had, of course, been established on their own farms when they married, because often the head of the family was then still a comparatively young man and was cultivating the original farm himself.

Victoria Square lay at the junction of two old carriage routes. A toll road ran east from Elgin Mills to meet the north-south road connecting Markham village and Stouffville. An antique shop is now located at what used to be the settlement of Cashel on Lot 26, Concession 6. When the building was constructed in 1840, it was first used as an inn, a stopping place for travellers on the route between Stouffville and York.

Early road construction was often undertaken by private companies who built the road, and then exacted payment for it by means of toll gates. It is said that the Markham-Stouffville section contained a toll gate which split the farm of the Raymer family, and the latter had to pay a toll in order to reach their back fields.

The Cashel road was of plank construction, one stage of improvement from log roads, the sequence in road building being usually blazed trails, trails cleared of stumps, a corduroy or log road, and then a plank road with toll gates. The planks provided smoother travelling than logs, but the roads were narrow and passing was hazardous to say the least. Cashel's hotel was doubtless a haven for many a weary traveller. The main room, which was the pub, shows evidence of the fireplace and bar which welcomed him with warmth for both his exterior and interior. The severity of life in pioneer days was alleviated by the construction of the inns; not only were they used by travellers, but almost every farmer was within walking distance of one such centre of social life.

Major John Button, who came from the Hudson Valley in 1810, raised a cavalry troop, the First Regiment of York Militia, one of the first volunteer units in Upper Canada. The land at Lot 16, Concession 4, was given to him as a reward after the War of 1812, and

The Cashel Hotel

Former wagon shop,
Button property

Buttonville bears his name. In the years following the war, Major
Button and his troop made a colourful picture at parades in York.
As Henry Scadding observes in *Toronto of Old*, 'and then in addition to the local cavalry corps there was the clattering scabbards,
blue jackets and bearskin helmets of Major Button's Dragoons from
Markham and Whitchurch.' The original house no longer stands on
Major Button's land, but the present board-and-batten frame house
was built by his son, Francis Button, before 1860. In the wagon
shop on the property (now an antique store) is a wheel with pulleys
which gave power for the lathe and drill for carriage repairs. The
floor dips from the weight of the many horses who stood here.
Across from the Button house is the James Walker home, built in
1858, of solid brick with quoining on the sides, and still in good
condition.

8

Vaughan Township

The early settlement of Vaughan Township was part of the general migration, with a preponderance of Germans from Pennsylvania, into Upper Canada in the 1790s and early 1800s. These first immigrants were followed by settlers from the British Isles, many of whom were craftsmen rather than farmers, and some of whom were millers by trade. From 1820 to 1840 many villages were started, always around a mill. They followed much the same growth pattern: the sawmill would shortly be followed by a grist mill, then a cooper, general store, blacksmith, church, school, tavern, wagon shop, and perhaps a woollen mill and distillery.

The varied cultures blended in Vaughan Township are evident in its early architecture. The first house of the Pennsylvania Germans was typically a log building which was soon extended into a house - perhaps frame or brick - which had one section for the parents when they turned over the operation of the farm to the next generation (the 'doddy' house, as noted earlier). Near the main house was a separate summer kitchen. There was also usually a separate brick bake-oven, and probably a workshop where articles were made and repaired. The barn was usually a 'bank' barn, built into the bank or hillside, and was always provided with an overhang to shelter cattle while feeding.

The houses of the settlers of English origin were usually built of brick and comfortably furnished. Because many of these immigrants had money, they endeavoured to duplicate the English properties they had left behind by means of landscaping and other such amenities. As they were unused to having to shelter animals during the winter months, many of their early barns resembled sheds.

The Scottish settlers tended to build stone houses because many of them were stonemasons by trade, and this material lay at hand in the fields and streams.

The fertile and hence highly desirable southeast corner of Vaughan Township was settled early by the Pennsylvania Germans. In 1816, after emigrating from Somerset County, Pennsylvania, with his grandfather, Jonathan Baker purchased Lot 11, Concession 2E, between Bathurst and Dufferin streets (1150 Langstaff Road). The original grant of this property had been to Daniel Cozens, a retired soldier, in 1801.

Baker cleared his acreage quickly and built a typical German barn in 1822, with the date emblazoned on the front. A log smoke-house dates from the 1820s. In the 1840s he built a small board-on-board house for his nephew, which was later used as a workshop. In 1853, Baker replaced the original crude log cabin with the present red brick house. All the woodwork, cupboards, and trim inside the house are of pine. There are wooden pegs in the walls for coats, small window-panes, and a rail of wood about three feet from the floor along the kitchen wall. The house is divided down the middle so that it could be used by two families; two separate front doors lead into the kitchens. About 1853, two summer kitchens were built, one containing the original bake-oven. In 1860, a driving-shed was added.

The family still has in its possession the Conestoga wagon which brought their ancestors from Pennsylvania (one of only two known to be preserved in Ontario). In 1860, when Jonathan Baker died childless, his nephew, Jonathan Baker Jr, carried on the farm and today the farm is still owned by his descendants. As the farm grew, additions were made of sheds and pens. As a result, the farm is almost totally self-sufficient today.

The Bakers were Tunkers, and belonged to a congregation organized in 1808. At first, various families took turns having meetings in their kitchens. The funeral of Jonathan Baker Jr's first wife was held in the driving-shed, and a 'lovefeast' (communion) was held in the barn on several occasions. The first local meeting-house, known as the Cober Church, was built in 1888 on the Baker-Cober property line, and still stands on Dufferin Street above the Langstaff Road. It continues to be used for services and funerals.

The Conestoga wagon which carried the Bakers from Pennsylvania in 1816

Jonathan Baker's barn, built 1822

The Baker smokehouse

Board-on-board house, built by Jonathan Baker in the 1840s

The Bakers' second house, built 1853

The time-lapse between the settlement of Jonathan Baker's property in 1816 and the building of the Tunker church is 60 years. The significance of this gap is that the congregation did not consider the structure of a church building of prime importance; over the years some sixteen different families alternated in setting up pine benches in their kitchens to accommodate the congregation.

One of the earliest churches in Vaughan Township was built, however, by Pennsylvania Germans in 1824. It is located at Edgeley, on the east side of Jane Street north of Highway 7, and is in good repair. The interior is of beautiful unpainted white pine. The rails, door handles, and door latches were all made by a local blacksmith. The first roof was finished with shingles two feet long or more, split from pine blocks and shaved with a draw-knife. The original log structure was covered in 1848 with wood siding. Many early settlers lie in the nearby cemetery, with old stones marking

Mennonite Church, Edgeley

their graves. Services in the meeting-house are now held only occasionally.

The area around the town of Maple offers several examples of different types of pioneer architecture. On the east side of Dufferin Street, just south of Major Mackenzie Drive (Lot 20, Concession 2W) stands a substantial brick house, 'Folly Farm,' painted white, classic in design, and reportedly built in the 1830s, although minor additions were made to it in 1880. This house has interesting semi-circular transom lights cut in the roof over what was the original front door on the north side and over the present front door on the west side. It overlooks the Don River, which flows through the property. The original builder is unknown, but in 1865 the property was listed as belonging to William Graham.

On the north side of Major Mackenzie Drive, between Dufferin and Bathurst, is a house built of board and batten with ornamented

'Folly Farm,' Maple

1078 Major Mackenzie Drive, built by Peter Patterson

pointed arches and gable ends. It is considered to be one of Vaughan Township's showplaces. The house was built about 1850 by Peter Patterson who, with his brothers, established the Patterson Farm Implement Company on the property. The blacksmith instrument foundry (now the barn), was built in 1847. The business continued there until 1891 when it was moved to Woodstock and shortly afterwards purchased by Massey-Harris. The now extinct town of Patterson grew up around the foundry and included over one hundred houses for the foundry workers, a blacksmith shop, machine shop, storage warehouse, lumber yard, office building, grist mill, school, church, stores, and post office. Only three or four of the old foundry workers' houses which were built between 1847 and 1850 remain on the property. The old blacksmith foundry is now used for cattle. The cattle graze and the Don River flows past where the busy 'company town' of Patterson once stood. The Pattersons had expected that the railroad would pass through their property when

The O'Brien Regency cottage

the roadbed was laid in 1853. Instead, it went through Maple, an event which determined the decline of Patterson.

One-half mile south of the Patterson buildings is a Regency cottage, one of the few remaining examples in Ontario of this romantic and beautiful style. It was standing in 1830, a simple utilitarian cabin which Edward O'Brien, an Irish naval officer, had built and was occupying. In the spring of that year, however, it became the home of Mary Gapper O'Brien when she married Edward. In her diary, *The Journals of Mary O'Brien*, she records the alterations Edward made in the house as it was reconstructed to its present form in preparation for their wedding:

... I am to be married the second week in May, and in truth I am well pleased that it should be so. Edward's solitary visits to his own house begin to grow irksome to him and I often find reasons why I should be with him.

The alterations are to be as follows: the door is to be moved to the west side next to the kitchen, which is to be made in the new part of the house. The chimney now standing is to be moved into it and replaced by a window. Then the whole is to be plastered at once to dislodge the present inhabitants, and the whole of the floor relaid.

At 339 Major Mackenzie Drive, just east of the CNR tracks at Keele Street, stands a one-storey fieldstone cottage started in 1837 by the Porter brothers and completed one year later. Construction was delayed because the two men were jailed over the winter months as a result of their support of William Lyon Mackenzie. The house is very spacious, with two parlours, dining-room, kitchen, and four bedrooms. A double fireplace is set between the dining-room and living-room, one side serving each room. A bell tower on the original summer kitchen was used to call for help in emergencies from neighbourhood farms. When the railway went through in 1853, it crossed the orchard at the front of the house. A descendant of the second owner recalls nearby Dufferin Street as a half-planked road, one side planked for full wagons on their way to market and the other side left in mud for the empty wagons on their return.

On Major Mackenzie Drive, between Keele and Jane streets, a red brick octagonal house stands on Lot 21, Concession 4. It was built about 1840 by Jacob Rupert, a Pennsylvania German. Octagonal buildings had become a fad during the mid-19th century through the influence of an American phrenologist and writer on many subjects, Orson Squire Fowler. He held that life in eight-sided houses improved the temper of the occupants because of the greater amount of light admitted and the easier housekeeping which he claimed would be possible. The rooms of the Rupert house are pie-shaped. Rupert is rumoured to have said himself that he built a round house so the devil could not corner him in it! All the lumber for the house was cut on the property, the bricks were made on the site, and the wood interior trim was cut by the Rupert daughters. Unfortunately, the house has deteriorated, but it remains of interest architecturally.

In the Woodbridge area are many examples of early buildings representative of the pioneer period. On the west side of Weston Road, south of Rutherford Road, is a simple frame house built in 1837 by Arthur McNeil, an Irish immigrant. The house is barn-shaped, with large windows and wide doors, and it is almost completely surrounded by a verandah. A large bin in an upstairs storeroom held the family's supply of flour. The house was built with plenty of

Octagonal house, Major Mackenzie Drive

closet space, which was unusual for that time. Around 1900, a small smoke-house was built to replace the original, and a summer kitchen with a bell-tower added.

On the east side of Highway 27, south of Rutherford Road, is the fieldstone house built by Henry Burton in 1860 for Andrew McClure. Burton was a Scottish stonemason who assisted in the construction of Osgoode Hall in Toronto. He built other fieldstone houses in the area: the John Jeffrey house, similar in plan to McClure's but a full two storeys, on Highway 7 at Woodbridge, and the Lawrie house on Highway 27 south of the tracks between Rutherford Road and the Langstaff Road, in the same year, 1860.

The enduring beauty of the work of another stonemason, yet unknown, is exemplified in a fieldstone house set back from the road on the south side of Teston Road on Lot 25, Concession 7, one and one-half miles east of Kleinburg. The builder, undoubtedly Scottish, was obviously skilled in his craft and the elevated setting of the

Frame house, Weston Road, built by Arthur McNeil

house displays the beauty of his workmanship. Although pioneers were usually forced to build their first home in haste, their permanent dwelling was often erected with great care over a period of years. In this instance, the 1851 census mentions a log cabin on the property and the 1861 census records the existence of a stone house – with 13 inhabitants!

Teston Road was originally the Purpleville Sideroad, adjacent to the village of Purpleville. Although most of the houses in these villages have vanished, their memories remain. The name of Purpleville seems to be either a reaction by non-sympathizers to the Orange Hall which was located beside the local blacksmith shop, or the village was named as a challenge to Orangeville, Ontario. Only the legends remain now. One is of the Purpleville woman who kept her own coffin in her home for twenty years before she died.

At 31 Clarence Street in Woodbridge is the original home of John Abell, a man of business who assisted in the development of the village. After settling in Burwick (now part of Woodbridge) in 1845, he started manufacturing wagons and carriages and constructed the first stage-coach that made regular trips between Toronto and Pine Grove. He manufactured one of the first grain separators in Canada and became the first reeve of Woodbridge. In 1850 Abell erected a two-storey frame house on the banks of the Humber River. One interesting feature is that the basement kitchen was connected to the dining-room on the main floor by a dumb-waiter.

Between the 7th and 8th concessions, just north of Woodbridge on Lot 11, Concession 8E, is a board-and-batten house with an unusual history. In 1836, John Edward Elliot purchased this property, which then included a log house, a barn, a trading-post (the present house) and a distillery. These buildings had formed a small squatters' settlement which was established as a half-way trading-post on the old Humber Trail, the earliest known access route to Vaughan Township. When Elliot purchased the farm, the squatters gave up possession peacefully and moved away. This marked the end of trading on the Humber Trail.

John Elliot, his wife and five children, lived in the log cabin for a time and then moved into the trading-post, which is the only building now left of this very old settlement. He later built a stone house beside it which was destroyed by fire in 1967. In 1837, William Lyon Mackenzie fled through Vaughan Township, crossing the footbridge over the Humber on the Elliot farm. Mackenzie described his flight:

We made for the Humber Bridge through Vaughan, but found it was strongly guarded; then we went up the river some distance, got supper at the house of a farmer, crossed the stream on a foot bridge [this was on the John Elliot farm] and by next morning reached the hospitable mansion of a worthy settler on Dundas Street, utterly exhausted and cold with fatigue.

The story goes that soldiers searched the Elliot buildings the next morning but found there only Mrs Elliot, who was confined to bed after the birth of a child.

One of the first pioneer families in the Kleinburg area was that of Joseph and Charlotte Capner, who came to Canada from England in 1830. Joseph Capner had been a gentleman farmer in England; in Canada he was faced with the necessity of clearing his land before even a log cabin could be built. At one point the family had to sell some of their clothing to obtain food.

The Capners, however, lived for 32 years on the bank of the

Elliot house, north of Woodbridge

Little Humber River in a log house, and there Mrs Capner bore ten children. She was a midwife and often travelled on horseback to deliver other women's babies. On one occasion, after she had helped deliver a child the father arrived home drunk, determined to go into his wife's bedroom. When he insisted, Mrs Capner took the whiskey bottle from his pocket and hit him over the head with it. He later took her before the magistrate in Woodbridge, who said, 'If there were more women like Mrs Capner in the world, there would be fewer men like you!'

In 1862, after so many years of hardship, the Capners built a substantial two-storey red brick house, which stands just south of Kleinburg on Islington Avenue.

Just inside the southern limits of Kleinburg, on the main street, is 'Redcroft,' a red brick house built in 1852 by Martin Smith. It has a pitched roof, peaked gable with inset window, and a porch

Capner house, just south of Kleinburg on Islington Avenue

with ornamental columns. Of particular interest are the tassels which ornament the verandah mouldings. This house is located near the old Indian trail that led through Kleinburg, providing a portage from the Humber River to Collingwood on the Nottawasaga River at Georgian Bay. The Smiths must have filled the house, for Martin had seventeen children. The farm originally covered 150 acres, a large part of which is now the McMichael Conservation Area.

On the south side of the Purpleville Sideroad (now Teston Road), west of Weston Road, stands a log house possibly dating from 1815, which was first used as a hunting lodge by Thomas Adams. Except for fieldstone facing on the east side, the house has had few alterations. It is interesting to note that it was built on the bank of a branch of the Humber River. Over the years the stream has cut away the bank and it now flows at the bottom of a steep ravine some distance from the house.

'Redcroft,' 10384 Islington Avenue, Kleinburg

Another well-known pioneer family, the Dalziels, came from Lanarkshire, Scotland, in 1828 and purchased a farm on Lot 1, Concession 5, from Johann Schmidt. On the Nashville Road, four miles west of Kleinburg, stands the fine brick house built in 1850 by John Dalziel, of the second generation of this family. The history of the Dalziels recounts that the first harvest of the original farm was wheat; Mrs Dalziel saved a small bag of grain from this first crop, which has been preserved by her descendants.

Also built by the Dalziel family is the 'Doctor's House' in Kleinburg, now a restaurant. When this simple frame building was a Dalziel home it was convenient to the nearby mill where its owner worked. It was later owned by Dr T.H. Robinson, born in 1850, who lived in the house from his graduation until his death. He visited his patients in the surrounding countryside in a buggy in summer and a cutter in winter. The house is in beautiful condition and dup-

John Dalziel's home, Nashville Road

licates the style seen so often in fieldstone in Vaughan. Here the finest in frame construction provides a striking comparison with the many stone houses in the region.

'Doctor's House,' Kleinburg

9

Whitchurch
Township

The name given to Whitchurch Township is of British origin. Some twelve towns or villages in England are called Whitchurch, the name being related to 'hwitan aerne' (white house in Old English), so called because built of stone.

There are indications that a large aboriginal population lived in Whitchurch before white settlers came. The *History of the County of York*, 1885, related that many Indian relics were found at Lot 9, Concession 8, 'on the brow of a hill overlooking a steep ravine,' and that at Lot 10, Concession 8, a pit with many hundreds of Indian skeletons was discovered in 1848. Excavating was done at Lot 16, Concession 6, and evidence found of still another Indian community. Three acres on top of the hill and part way down the slope were enclosed by a trench and a mound. The trench, five feet in depth, showed evidence of a wooden palisade. Originally, forest was cleared for a considerable distance around the village. Many of the pine trees growing there were forked at the root, showing that they must have been trodden down when young. A burying-ground was discovered outside the trench on the north side in which were 2000 graves, all made singly. This was unusual because the Huron Indian custom was to expose the corpse until the flesh was eaten by birds or beasts of prey and then to inter the bones in a common pit. The bodies in the single graves had been laid on their sides with the knees drawn up to the chins.

Whitchurch Township originally was laid out in 1780 by John Stegmann, an ex-officer in the Hessian Regiment during the War of

Independence who became government surveyor in Upper Canada. Settlers began to come in 1795, and the first patent for land was given to Joseph Bouchette in 1796. Some of the earliest holders of land were Huguenots from France, who first settled near Oak Ridges but did not remain. The first real colonizer was Timothy Rogers from Vermont, as noted in the chapter on Newmarket. He was offered 1000 acres of land in 1802 if he would persuade 40 settlers to come to this part of the province, and this he did. Many of the first settlers were Quakers from Pennsylvania. Rogers and Jacob Lundy took a leading part in the affairs of this group. Typical of their aims was a petition, presented to Lieutenant-Governor Francis Gore when he arrived in Upper Canada, which represents the Quakers as 'hoping thy administration may be such as to be a terror to the evil-minded and a pleasure to them that do well; then will the province flourish under thy direction.'

Three homes which belonged in the Lundy family are located close by each other, one on each of the 2nd, 3rd, and 4th concessions. A Lundy farm is located on Lot 34, Concession 4W; it was the property of William Lundy Sr. The brick house which stands on the property today was probably built about 1850. Six generations of Lundys have lived in this solid two-storeyed house, whose interior is relatively unchanged. Descendants of William Lundy tell of the family worshipping at the Pine Orchard Friends Meeting House. Family lore has it that one of their members assisted in carrying a coffin to its resting place in the grave when the horses refused to go into the churchyard. The horses' instinct was sound. En route to the grave an agitated thumping was heard from inside the sealed coffin - the erstwhile corpse was alive!

Enos Lundy, possibly a brother of Jacob, built his first home on Lot 26, Concession 3W, in 1808 and it still stands with even some of the original glass in the windows. It was built of solid pine logs which have been stuccoed over. In the kitchen a window-pane has scratched upon it the name of a descendant living in the house, 'H.T. Lundy, Sept. 6, 1858.' Lundy's was one of the very first log homes in the area. On Lot 26, Concession 2E, another house built and owned by Enos Lundy is located. It was to this house, built in 1828 of home-made bricks, that Enos moved twenty years after he had built his first home. Of the three Lundy houses, this is in the best state of preservation. Originally it had a verandah which has now disappeared. The bake-oven in the basement also was removed and replaced by a modern furnace. Among the many notable facts about this Pennsylvania Quaker family is that Enos was the great-grandfather of the novelist, Mazo de la Roche, author of the 'Jalna' novels.

The first ten or fifteen years of the 19th century, which saw the migration of several prominent Quaker families from Pennsylvania, are recalled in another early name, Widdifield. Henry Widdifield, who built the brick house on Lot 32, Concession 3E, called 'Maryvale Farms,' was the son of Mordecai Widdifield, who was living in Whitchurch and well established by 1809. Henry Widdifield gave the timber for the first meeting-house at Pine Orchard. 'Maryvale Farms' is of remarkably early date (1814) for such a substantial brick home, and is comparable with the home of William Lundy Sr on Lot 34, Concession 4W. Such early dates are unusual for two-storeyed homes of this size. It is far more common to find substantial homes erected twenty years or so later when the first log cabin

Enos Lundy home, Lot 26, Concession 2E, built in 1828

had become too small, the farm was well established and the family's struggle for existence easier. An interesting feature of the Widdifield house is the quarter-circle windows under the eaves.

Peter Brillinger was born in Pennsylvania in 1788 and came to Whitchurch in 1795. His son George was born in 1816, and the latter's brick home is located on Lot 3, Concession 4E. The door with its wide lights, the twelve-paned windows, and the verandah (now partly removed) tell its age. An old cemetery, located in front, contains early Brillinger graves.

The Barkey family, also from Pennsylvania, arrived between 1800 and 1810. Jacob Sr settled south of Ringwood on Highway 48. On Lot 3, Concession 7W, a home built (about 1850) by John Barkey, son of Jacob, shows a number of features common to early houses in the county such as the steep, sharply pointed gable, and the decorative brickwork on the front and at the corners. The panelling in the living-room of pine cut in the area is original.

John Bogart arrived in Upper Canada from Muncy, Pennsylvania, in 1802. In 1805 he built a sawmill in what was later called Bogarttown, and in 1830 put up a large frame mill at the then astronomical cost of $10,000. It was located on a stream flowing past the north-west corner of Concession 2 and the sideroad. Bits of the concrete foundation are still there, all that remained after fire destroyed the fine mill.

Bogart built his home on Lot 31, Concession 2, and lived near the mill until he moved to Newmarket. The first dwelling was a bark shelter. The Bogarts' second house was built of logs and served the family until 1811 when the present house was erected. The log house provided shelter and its door provided transportation: it could be removed to serve as a sled base for family trips – another example of the ingenuity of the early settlers. A white wrought-iron fence encloses Bogart's two-storey frame house (an addition at the rear is of brick). Four windows on the second storey are balanced by three windows and a door below. This is a variation on the more usual central placement of the door in early houses.

Bogarttown grew steadily and before the railroad came to Newmarket in the 1850s the village was a busier community than its neighbour. The arrival of the railroad in Newmarket seriously affected the growth of most villages in the vicinity, in particular Holland Landing and Bogarttown. One of the oldest schools in Ontario is the Bogarttown School on the Vivian Sideroad, Lot 31, Concession 3. Now the property of the Whitchurch Historical Society, it is used as a museum.

Jonathan Petch, the founding father of Petchville, settled soon after 1800 on Lot 21, Concession 3, where he built a log house which still stands. He was unable to buy this land until 1840, as the property was a Clergy Reserve and could only be leased. The Clergy Reserve lands had been set apart under the Constitutional Act of 1791 for the maintenance of 'a Protestant clergy' in Upper and Lower Canada, as noted earlier. Reservations of land for this purpose continued until 1838, at which time a total of 2,400,000 acres was held. In the early years, the rent for Reserves land was 10 shillings for 200 acres, but with the progress of settlement, the rents rose and became the subject of much complaint. The various Protestant churches also fought for their respective portions of these land rights for over thirty years. Eventually, some lands were sold in 1827, some in 1840, and all by 1854, when the Canadian Parlia-

John Bogart's third house, built 1811

ment voted that the proceeds of the sales be used by the municipal authorities for education.

But in 1840 Jonathan Petch received his land deed from the crown, paying £175. This granted him and his heirs the land forever 'saving nevertheless, all mines of silver and gold.' Petch's log house was made of logs 14 inches wide and 26 to 28 inches deep. The original house has been enlarged by the addition of a house moved from another concession. The window in the bedroom has been blocked off; this was the daughter's room and the purpose was to protect her from Indians. The marks of arrowheads, in fact, remain in some of the logs of the building. Petch had served at sea with Lord Nelson, but the wooden leg for which he was noted came not from a sea battle but from a fall off a cliff. He was a ship's carpenter who came to Canada from Yorkshire with his sister Rachel in the early years of the 1800s. After he was able finally to purchase his land, he gave one-half acre on the south-east corner of his lot

Jonathan Petch's log house

for the building of the Wesleyan Methodist Church. The old church was later moved to the Petch farm and forms part of the barn today.

The crossroad to the south of Petch's house was once known as Goosetown. On the south-east corner of this crossroad stands a pleasant house of board-on-board construction. It probably was built about 1850 but little is known of its history.

Colonel W.H. Beresford purchased Lots 30 and 31 on Concession 3 in Whitchurch, and on Lot 31 he built in 1840 'Pleasantview House.' Although it appears to be a single storey brick building, it does have rooms upstairs. An outstanding feature of the front door is the elliptical fan light whose curve is accentuated by a curved pattern of brick work that follows the same lines. Colonel Beresford built on the adjoining Lot 30 a house which unfortunately was destroyed but which in its day must have been a conversation piece. The three-feet thick walls, built of straw and mud (mud brick), enclosed 18 rooms, 7 fireplaces, and 45 doors.

Board-on-board, where Goosetown stood

On Lot 27, Concession 3, is the William Wallis home of brick, now painted white, built in 1855. Wallis was one of the first councillors of Newmarket. As his home has been renovated completely, some of the outside features are not as in the original. The front door is new but the simple transom remains; the off-centre placement of the door is puzzling. Interior floors and mouldings have been restored.

Two houses on Lot 19, Concession 3, recall the history of the notable Colonel William Graham, although the property passed into the Richardson family in 1830. After a distinguished military career, Colonel Graham settled in Nova Scotia but when John Graves Simcoe was appointed lieutenant-governor of Upper Canada, William Graham decided to relocate. The paths of the two men had crossed during the American campaign and Graham admired Simcoe. In 1794 Graham was appointed master carpenter to superintend the construction of the government buildings at York. He re-

William Wallis home

ceived a 3000-acre grant, mostly in Whitchurch, in recognition of his military service; during the war of 1812, he was colonel of the 1st Regiment of York Militia. His twin sons, Adam and Peter, who inherited the property after their older brother William died, were of totally different dispositions. Adam, the aggressive one, was active in the Mackenzie Rebellion and his name was on the 'wanted' list after the Rebellion was suppressed. Peter, a fine carpenter, was more peaceable and conservative, but such was their difference of views, that by their request a board fence was built to separate their graves in the family plot!

David Richardson bought the Graham land in 1830 and built about 1840 the lovely home that stands on Lot 19, Concession 3W. A verandah surrounds the house on three sides. This useful and common feature allowed the ladies to take their exercise without suffering from rain, mud, or snow. Its disadvantage was that it shaded the interior in winter. The entrances from the verandah are directly into the parlour and living-room. The house has no hallway, which is unusual. The other David Richardson home, on Lot 19E (1855), is a smaller brick building with a pointed gable with decorative barge-board.

The Van Nostrand family, who built the frame house on Lot 17, Concession 4W, were descended from a family of Long Island, New York. John Van Nostrand went to Whitchurch to farm in 1854, built his home and acquired 1300 acres of land. He owned a large lumber business and a sawmill, also located on Lot 17, Concession 4. He manufactured annually about one million feet of lumber, giving employment to over twenty men.

Van Nostrand, like other sawmill owners, was a mainstay of the local hamlet. In the 1840s the county had 59 gristmills and 186 sawmills. The pattern of settlement here as elsewhere can be spelled out in terms of mills - first came the settler with capital and knowledge who built the expensive sawmill; a gristmill followed next to supply the settlers with ground flour; these enterprises led to a commercial flour mill, then to a general store, and then to the cooper, needed to make barrels. The all-important mills were nevertheless hazardous to operate, subject to ravages by flood, fire, low water, and loss of market. Men such as Van Nostrand were among the first successful industrial entrepreneurs in Upper Canada. Many of them later became promoters of banks, railroads, and insurance companies.

Although later in date than the houses just mentioned (as it was rebuilt in 1870), the house on Lot 2, Concession 7W, contains fine stonework. It was constructed from the original James Lee house built in 1831. Its exterior presents an unusual combination of brick and colourful stonework. The brick is used to accent the door and windows and to provide a pattern along the sides.

In the Samuel Brownsberger home, Lot 2, Concession 8W, the brick work is also accented with patterning. The house's most notable feature, however, is the door which is of generous proportions and restates the axiom so important in this age - hospitality. Often more time and expense were spent on the door than on any other part of the house as it represented the desire for company to lighten the harsh pioneer routine.

Restoration can be accomplished without altering the quality of early buildings, and a fine example is the Robert Stapleton home on Lot 8, Concession 8E. Built of stone in 1862, it has the original shutters and a cedar-shake roof. The house has been added to twice:

Fine stonework: Lot 2, Concession 7W

first, a brick winter kitchen and living area, and second, a stone summer kitchen and storage shed. A dormer also has been added to provide extra light for the second floor. The summer kitchen contains a large fireplace wide enough to hold two swinging arms for kettles and a flue big enough to hold a man. The bake-oven has been restored. Upstairs, where there are now four bedrooms, the original had just one room. A partition divided the boys' section from the girls' section, and each sex had separate stairways which the restoration has preserved.

The Robert Fenton home on Lot 6, Concession 9W, was built by the British government for its 'land overseer.' The windows and leaded door lights show superb early craftsmanship and the brick is in an excellent state of repair. Inside the house the bee cupboards are an interesting feature: in poor weather the bees were brought in to the second floor and placed in the double cupboard, which had air holes and accommodation for the owner to reach in and remove the honey.

As elsewhere in York County, the names of early settlements in Whitchurch have lingered long after those communities suffered a regression in settlement, either as a result of the railroad by-passing them, or the moving of inhabitants to larger centres. Old names still retain significance for local residents, and Whitchurch has many that are affectionately recalled. Nelson Patterson was chiefly responsible for the existence of Bloomington. At one time its expansion merited the designation of a 'Blooming Town,' later changed to Bloomington. Lemonville derived its name from George Lemon, as did Petchville from Jonathan Petch. In the 19th century Lemonville was a village of 200 inhabitants. Now it is half the size. However, names have staying-power. In the case of Bloomington, the town may have vanished but Bloomington Sideroad recalls its existence.

10

King Township

King Township, located in the north-west corner of York County, is fortunate to possess probably more well-maintained or tastefully renovated early buildings than any other township in the county.

Named after Major John King, an English Under-Secretary of State, King is also the largest township in the county. The first survey was made in 1800 by Stegmann, but although most of the area was highly suited to agriculture, it was not until well into the 1820s that it began to attract any considerable amount of settlement. The first portions to be occupied were along Yonge Street and north-west towards Kettleby. The majority of early settlers had been Americans, many of them United Empire Loyalists, but later on new arrivals came increasingly from Great Britain.

Kettleby has been by-passed by highway construction so that many of its old buildings are still standing. In 1825 one hundred acres of property including a wide ravine and a stream were bought by Jacob Tool of Pennsylvania. He utilized the water power to build a sawmill which stood on the site until it burned in 1950. It was not until 1842, however, that Kettleby's development gained momentum with the arrival of Septimus Tyrwhitt, who bought 46 acres of Tool's property. He embarked immediately on plans for other mills and employed many men and scores of teams of oxen to cut and burn timber. When the day came for raising his mill, men came from far and near and huge kettles were brought to prepare the food. One local legend maintains that the name 'Kettle Bee' derived from this construction bee. It seems more probable, however, that Mrs Tyrwhitt named the village Kettleby after the place in Wales where her husband was raised. In 1852 Septimus Tyrwhitt became reeve of King Township.

Unfortunately, none of the early mills remain as they were damaged by a series of floods and fires, and finally the advent of the railway took industrial development elsewhere. One house, built in 1843 by Jacob Tool of mud brick baked on the property, still stands on Lot 28, Concession 4, on the north side of Main Street.

The village grew rapidly in the 1840s and soon became a thriving centre, with hotel-keepers, blacksmiths, shoemakers, tailors, coopers, potash boilers, harness-makers, carriage-makers, whiskey distillers, builders, and related artisans. The present Main Street retains the character of early days with several buildings of pre-Confederation date built by original settlers. The Walton family was responsible for several of the buildings that remain, including the general store. Jacob Walton, formerly of Newmarket, had been apprenticed to the trade of blacksmith, and worked at that occupation for ten years. He was the son of Jesse Walton of New Brunswick, from a family of United Empire Loyalists. In Kettleby he became a general merchant, and postmaster in 1853. The store originally was attached to the house on its west side, and the present owners believe that the buildings were separated in the early days because the two owners at the time held strongly opposing views on drinking habits. The Walton house was then moved several feet to the west.

Kettleby was one of the strongholds of the temperance movement in the mid-19th century – in fact, it had the largest membership in all of Ontario in its Sons of Temperance Society. The distillery was built in 1843 and the total abstinence society formed six years later in 1849. At this time King Township supported seventeen places licensed for the sale of liquor. Kettleby itself had two hotels – while the more than two hundred members of the Temperance Society steadfastly maintained allegiance to their pledge. The Temperance Hall, built in 1850, is now in Black Creek Pioneer Village.

The minutes of a King Township agricultural society note that at a meeting the usual toasts were drunk: 'The Queen – three times; Prince Albert and the Royal Family – three times; and the Governor General – three times.' At the conclusion of the session the minutes record that all were much pleased with the business of the day and with each other.

Just north of Kettleby, close to Highway 400, is a pocket of six early buildings. Four of these are exceptionally fine houses. On Lot 32, Concession 4E, is the Thomas Cosford home which was built about 1832. This particularly fine stone house, built in the Georgian style, originally had a verandah extending across the front. The present second-storey windows were a later addition. These alterations have not spoiled the attractive lines of the house. The original floors remain and are of one and one-half inch tongue-and-groove planks. Most of the floors downstairs are of oak, probably taken from the property and milled in Kettleby. The remaining floors are of pine. The walls are of solid stone two feet thick. Cosford was a substantial citizen, contributing to the life of his community as school commissioner and councillor.

Directly across the road from the Cosford house, on Lot 32, Concession 3W, stands another fine stone building. It was probably the work of the same builder as the Cosford house, for they are similar in many respects. 'Stoneleigh' (the Gaelic word for field being

Thomas Cosford home, north of Kettleby

'leigh') was built in 1858. A recent addition at the rear, while modern in design, retains the flavour of the early portion of the house. The stones on the front of the house are larger than those on the sides and back, and they have a flat surface; this creates a more imposing appearance and was doubtless done to put the best face forward to the road.

The William Mason frame house located on Lot 31, Concession 5E, stands on land which was bought from King's College (later the University of Toronto) in 1851. The house was built shortly thereafter and became a centre of social activities for King Christian Church, which is now Emmanuel Baptist Church on Lot 34, Concession 5E. Many neighbourhood gatherings took place here, such as the strawberry festivals which were held once a year and were known far and wide. Often as many as six hundred people were served supper in the spacious grounds surrounding the house, to the accompaniment of a brass band. The interior of the house has been

'Stoneleigh,' north of Kettleby

almost completely restored to its original state by private owners.

One of the largest houses in the Kettleby district is that of Elisha Chappel on Lot 34, Concession 4. Of uncertain date, it probably was built in the mid-19th century. Large columns in the front, which give a classical look, were a later addition but otherwise the house is unchanged.

To the south of Kettleby, on Lot 25, Concession 4, is 'Springdale,' originally a 200-acre property situated in the area which was once called the 'Mountains of King.' The large Georgian-style brick house on the property was built in 1843 by John Webb. Webb came to Upper Canada in 1806 and when he married in 1819, decided to buy property for a farm. This area near Kettleby was developing quickly because of the many mills located near by. This house seems remarkably substantial in view of the fact that the Webbs were Quakers who did not believe in any form of ostentation. The Quakers did, however, believe in excellence and the quality of the mate-

William Mason house, near Kettleby

rials in this house attests to this. The house is in superb condition today. A portico, added at a later date, gives an impressive air to this fine home.

John Webb's son Ira, who had been a teacher, became a farmer and miller in 1849 and built a sawmill on the property. Although the Kettleby area held many mills, they were geared to the export trade. Webb's mill was built to supply a local market. It thrived, and in December 1867 he made a trip to Toronto to purchase a piece of casting for the mill. Missing the train, he walked the 25 miles to his home in King, carrying the casting. He reached his destination, but died shortly thereafter from a heart attack.

The year 1837 was one of increasing political agitation by William Lyon Mackenzie and his followers. Meetings were held throughout the county as his supporters became more incensed. One of the most important meetings was held in Lloydtown, where Mackenzie, Samuel Lount, Jesse Lloyd, and David Gibson, all important leaders

Elisha Chappel house, Lot 34, Concession 4

of the Rebellion, spoke. Lloyd was one of Mackenzie's most trusted lieutenants. A leader in his community and a wealthy man by the standards of the day, he became a hero of the Rebellion. He acted as a courier between Mackenzie and Louis Joseph Papineau, the leader of the Rebellion in Lower Canada.

Jesse Lloyd had emigrated in 1812 from Pennsylvania to King Township where he built a saw and gristmill at Lloydtown. Shortly thereafter he purchased more land and proceeded to develop it. However, he became so committed to Mackenzie and the Rebellion that he decided to devote his full energy to this cause. Lloyd's participation in the conflict against the Family Compact, however, caused his expulsion from the Quaker congregation, loss of wealth and health, and an exile's death in Ohio at the age of 53. After his hasty departure following the skirmish at Montgomery's Tavern, his wife Phoebe was left to raise thirteen children and an infant grandchild. She lived the rest of her life in dire poverty, oppressed

'Springdale,' south of Kettleby

One of King's few early frame houses, built by Thomas Hall in 1845

The Hall house, south-west of Lloydtown

by opponents of her husband's cause. She died at the age of 89 in 1882 and her grave may be seen today in the Lloydtown cemetery. The inscription on her gravestone reads:

Jesus has called the mother home,
Her flesh lies mouldering in the tomb.
God grant her offspring will be blest
And meet her in eternal rest.

Recently the King Township Council began a careful restoration of the cemetery.

Across from the Anglican cemetery is a small house which was built originally around 1825 as a powder magazine; it is constructed of timbers twelve inches thick, now covered with insulbrick.

To the south-west of Lloydtown are scattered a number of well-preserved early homes. One of the few early frame houses in King is located on Lot 28, Concession 12E. It was built in 1845 by Thomas Hall, a builder and carpenter from Toronto. Hall was an English immigrant who came first to Toronto, and being a skilled carpenter, worked on the Parliament Buildings there before moving to King Township. He was a farmer, and owned a thriving lumber business as well. During a complete renovation of the Hall house in 1946, the walls were stripped and every board replaced. Imaginative use was made of the stone foundations of the old barn, which were incorporated into an informal garden. The former silo, with its cone-shaped roof, is now the garden shed. The extensive restoration has been well conceived and executed, particularly considering that when the present owner took possession of the house, cows were wandering through the building.

Typical of many of the stone houses in the area is the George Burton home in the middle of Lot 26, Concession 11. It was built by a Scottish stonemason who came to Canada in 1840 and is said to have built fifty stone houses within a twenty-five-mile area. The plan of the Burton house is probably the most common in York County: it has a centred door flanked by two twelve-paned windows, a sloped roof, and balanced chimneys. The house is of field-stone from the area and remains in excellent condition. Tragedy is associated with its history, however, complete with a family ghost. While driving a team of horses one day, George Burton's 12-year-old son lost control of the team. As one of the horses reared, Burton came to his son's aid. He hurled a pitchfork at the animal but hit and killed his son instead. Following this tragedy, Burton's wife left home and shortly thereafter Burton left also. He went to Australia, where he made a fortune, returning in later years to the Schomberg area, although not to this house. For years the house stood empty and area residents believed it to be haunted by the boy's ghost. In 1859 George Burton gave one acre of his property to the Congregational Church for use as a cemetery which can still be seen on the east corner of Lot 26, Concession 11. Burton himself is buried in the cemetery.

Near by, at Thomson Lake on Lot 20, Concession 10, is the original Thomson home, 'Bladesover.' Born in England, Thomson came to Canada in 1836, located near Lloydtown, and later bought property on both the 9th and 10th concessions. The house retains one-half of the original 200-acre crown grant. Built of fieldstone, it still has the original pine floor.

George Burton house, Lot 26, Concession 11

Of even earlier vintage, 1828, is the William McDevitt house to the east on Lot 23, Concession 8. It was built by Scottish labourers, from mail-order catalogue plans, using stones from the property. McDevitt was Irish and had begun life as a shoemaker. The upper floor of the house has no access from front to back; the theory is that the front was used exclusively by the parents and daughters while the back was used by sons and travellers.

Anthony Hollingshead, a United Empire Loyalist, was the original owner of 'Overdown' Farm on Lot 1, Concession 8. Born in 1800, he was present at the Battle of York where, it is said, he drove, at the age of 12, a wagon-load of American prisoners. The interior woodwork of his brick house (of pre-1855 date) shows the combined skills of him and his five sons, some of whom were carpenters by trade. At one time the house had a verandah but this has been removed and now the symmetrical facade is unadorned, but enhanced by a fieldstone wall.

Christopher Stokes house, Mill Road

Born in 1800 and a miller by trade, Christopher Stokes emigrated to Canada in 1827, bought 200 acres of land, and built a gristmill at King Creek in the 1830s. His home on Lot 4, Concession 7, was built in 1835 and has been much altered since; it is all that remains of the once thriving settlement of 'King Creek.' The main portage from Lake Simcoe to Toronto crossed the Humber at this place but the village disappeared with the coming of the railway. Many of the original features of the Stokes house can still be seen; the front door and windows are clues to its age.

Stokes was an industrious settler. His mill was highly successful and it served farmers who had no other way to bring their grain than by carrying it on their backs. On his death Stokes left an estate of $30,000 to testify to his industry.

The town of Laskay was situated on the banks of the Humber in the 6th Concession of King Township. It was just east of the old Indian Trail, the 'Toronto Carrying Place.' This trail enabled travel

'The Old Forge,' north of Laskay

by canoe from Lake Simcoe to Lake Ontario, but included a 28-mile portage from the Holland River to the mouth of the Humber on Lake Ontario. At that time the Humber was full of salmon – which were fed to the oxen. The present Highway 400 parallels roughly this route. The name Laskay was given to the settlement by Joseph Baldwin after his native home, Loskie, in Yorkshire, England. A subsequent nickname, 'Bulltown,' came from a disaster at a Fall Fair when a bull broke loose and charged the crowd. The present hotel was built by Baldwin as his home. The two-storey verandah was added when it became a hotel. The Laskay Emporium was originally situated next door to the hotel; it has now been removed to Black Creek Pioneer Village and restored.

When Baldwin first settled at Laskay the property he had purchased was still covered by forest with the exception of the beginning of a sawmill, the work of a previous owner. He completed the work and operated his mill on the branch of the Humber. A man

'Kinghaven Farms,' King Sideroad

St Andrew's Church, Strange

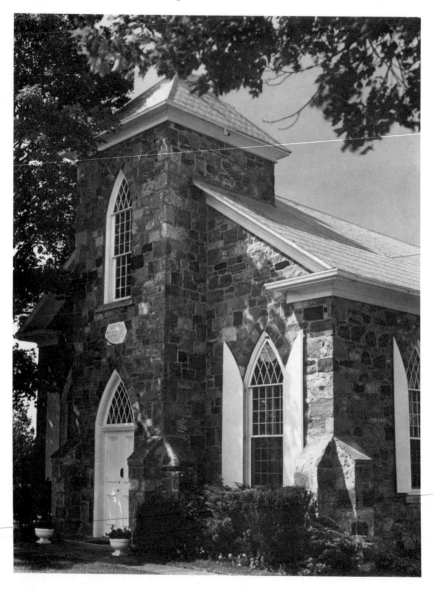

of immense energy, Baldwin cleared his land, operated the mill, represented the township in the district council, and built flour and grist mills.

North of Laskay is a house known as the 'Old Forge.' It was originally the property of Daniel O'Brien, son of William O'Brien of Nova Scotia. William was a keen supporter of Mackenzie but managed to escape capture after the Rebellion. While his house was searched on many occasions, he was always warned in time to go into hiding. Daniel O'Brien was a blacksmith; hence his house's name. Built in 1858, the house has also been used as an inn. It has been tastefully and authentically restored.

On Lot 5, Concession 6, on the south side of King Sideroad, and west of 'Old Forge,' is the Frederick Willis house built in 1831. It is called 'Kinghaven Farms.' The rear wing, added at a later date, is an exact replica of the original house which was built of the beautiful local fieldstone.

St Andrew's Presbyterian Church at Strange was built in 1860, replacing a hewn pine log church which dated from 1837. Ministers would travel by horseback to their various preaching posts, often many miles apart, but in 1860 St Andrew's received the remarkable Dr Carmichael, who preached two services a day, one in English, and the other in Gaelic for his Scottish flock. In 1960 a service of deconsecration was held at the church in order for it to be used as a home. It still retains the high arched windows, 20-foot ceiling, and some of the pews. The exterior remains unaltered.

The General Store in King City is in fine condition and dates back to about 1863. An old-fashioned general store such as this was a necessity for any pioneer community. It sold nearly everything: hardware, dry goods, horse blankets, harness, boots, tools, coal-oil, lamps, dishes, and groceries. In addition, it was a social centre. The interior of the King City store has changed little over the years and it is one of the very few remaining genuine country stores in Ontario. A film has been produced using King City as the location and the General Store in particular as the setting, since its atmosphere so perfectly recalls the days when Ben Lloyd built it.

Across from the General Store, is the old inn, of red brick painted white, formerly called 'Hogan's at Four Corners.' Built soon after 1851, for nearly fifty years Hogan's was the most important inn in King Township. The dining-room and kitchen were in the basement; the travellers' sample rooms and bar on the first floor. The stables were next door with a dance hall attached: 'Gentlemen $1.00, ladies free, lunch served!' It is reported that for a while the old building served two differing functions: while serving its customers as a licensed house downstairs, it was the location for the services of All Saints Anglican Church upstairs. The verandah has been removed, revealing the fan transom above the door.

The carefully restored log house on Lot 2, Concession 2E, was built in approximately 1820 but the builder is unknown. It is large for a log house, 24 × 28 feet, and at one time may have been a schoolhouse. The interior is tastefully decorated in pine. The huge logs used in its construction are exposed. Indian arrowheads and skinning knives have been found near the square-timbered building, indicating that an Indian camp may have been located there.

The 1840 house of Charles Grant on Lot 3, Concession 2E, is located on what was part of the Clergy Reserves. The front door of

General Store, King City

the Grant house is original, as are the windows and the walnut banister inside; the dormers are a later addition. The interior is a mixture of Georgian and Colonial styles, with high ceilings. Over the old glass panes of the door and each window is a finely carved shelf. At one time during its history, the house was turned 180 degrees on its foundation. This was done because the wife of the owner objected to seeing the barn from her front door. Her obliging husband turned the house for her, which explains why the 'front' of the house faces north, away from the barn on the south.

The James Thompson house, Lot 10, Concession 2, looks exactly as it did when built. The crown grant had been made to Archibald Thompson as early as 1797 so the date of construction is uncertain. It could be the 1830s. The first floor has two large rooms, with a hall and stairway in the back. This is another example of the fine craftsmanship in stonework seen in King Township, and the high

Front door, Grant house

quality of the native fieldstone. The Thompson house is in the Temperanceville School area in which a particularly strong community spirit existed in the early 19th and mid-19th century. The community was the centre for five different temperance societies between 1840 and 1890 and so derived its name.

The little village of Eversley on the 3rd Concession of King about one mile north of King Sideroad at one time boasted a cheese factory and the 'Misses Gellatly's' store, plus a public school and church, a blacksmith's, and a wheelwright's. The name is believed to have come from a small village in England where Charles Kingsley, author of *Westward Ho*, was curate. The one outstanding example of the past in Eversley is St Andrew's Presbyterian Church, which exists through the generosity of Lady Eaton who, a few years ago, bought and preserved it in honour of the community's early pioneers. The original hewn-log building was both church and school until St Andrew's was built in 1848. The property on which the church was

St Andrew's Church, Eversley

built was sold to the community for 'five pounds of lawful money' by Joseph Wells, head of a distinguished family which made contributions to their country in politics, law, and medicine.

A substantial house for its age is that of Timothy Rogers on Lot 11, Concession 2. It is on the site of an early Indian encampment. The present building, which, judging by the woodwork, has been dated 1850, is unaltered and includes maids' quarters and a staircase with crescent windows on the side. The dining-room has classical mouldings and the original pine floors remain. The owner of this remarkable mansion in the bush was the son of James Rogers, who emigrated to Canada from Vermont with his father Timothy. He took 200 acres of bushland and made a fine farm for his wife and nine children.

Neighbours of the Rogers were the William Davis family, also from the United States, who petitioned for land in Upper Canada in 1793 and took up residence later in a brick house, built in 1846

Timothy Rogers house

on Lot 10, Concession 3E. Many changes have been made to this house, most noticeably the addition of dormers.

To the north, on Lot 13, Concession 2W, is the historic 'Eversley Farm,' which has stood at the end of a winding road since the turn of the 18th century. In 1939 the house was sold including 120 acres of land. When the new owner instructed his workmen to pull down the roughcast plaster structure, he was told that they had found beneath the surface a log house which resisted demolition. What they had found was the home built of logs in the 1790s by Daniel Rose of the Queen's Rangers. He had been granted 400 acres of land by Governor Simcoe for services rendered. The crown deed registered in 1797 refers to a 'house built of logs.' The logs still in this building are squared white pine. The logs were covered with plaster in the 1800s and remained that way until their rediscovery in 1929. The new owner preserved the original broad axe which had hewn the white pine.

Patrick Hartney house, once a hotel

A crown grant to James Fulton in 1803 for the land on Lot 21, Concession 2, on the north side of township road 15, brought another pioneer to this area. The present stucco-over-brick house probably was built in the early 1800s. At one time a sawmill was operated from the pond and there were beaver dams in the stream above and below the pond. This house has been maintained carefully through the years by a succession of owners.

North of the Kettleby area and east on Lots 1 and 2, Concession 2, north of Highway 9, is the Patrick Hartney house. The date 1825 has been found on a beam in the basement. The house has been renovated extensively but the windows in the old central part are original and the panes and mullions are irregular in size. Upstairs, the pine floors remain. Now called 'March Winds,' this house was once a hotel, and rumour has it that for a time it was a house of ill repute.

11

East Gwillimbury Township

The first survey of East Gwillimbury was made in 1800 by John Stegmann, and the township was given its name in honour of Governor Simcoe's father-in-law, Major Gwillim, who had been aide-de-camp to General Wolfe and died in the battle of the Plains of Abraham. The War of 1812 gave a spurt to development of the township. Soldiers's Bay, on the east side of the Holland River, north of the Queensville Sideroad, was a busy supply depot. Soldiers were billeted in local homes. The increased demand for food opened up new land and encouraged agricultural activity but when the demand disappeared after the war, development slowed.

The best known landmark in East Gwillimbury is the Temple of the Children of Peace at Sharon, founded by David Willson. Willson came to Sharon, then called Hope, in 1803 and settled on Lot 10, Concession 2. He was then a Presbyterian but as a sailor had travelled extensively in China and the far east, where he became intensely interested in mysticism and symbolism. This was to be an important influence in the construction of the Temple at Sharon.

Willson joined the Quakers when he settled at Sharon and for several years was their schoolmaster, instructing with all the fervour that later made his speeches so spellbinding. The Quakers were hard-working honest people who opposed all ostentation, social or verbal. Their meeting house and rituals were simple; there was no sermon, pulpit or scripture reading, and certainly no music. The Friends simply sat quietly and meditated.

David Willson was moved one day to an outburst of joy - 'Let

The Temple of the Children of Peace, Sharon

every heart with joy abound like David's harp of solemn sound.'
'Sit thee down, David!' an elder commanded him, but Willson did
not hold his peace. At the next meeting he was expelled from the
Society. Five families withdrew with him. Willson said, 'I had many
visitations that I might speak of the Lord in assemblies ... to arise
and speak of the Lord in the society of Quakers, of which I was
then a member in good esteem ... But oh! the disappointment that
followed my few words of utterance cannot be conceived ... Their
love to me became hatred and condemnation rose where justifica-
tion had been.'

The five families, with David Willson as their leader, established
at Hope the Church of the Children of Peace. The name of Hope
was changed to Sharon, for the plain known for its fertility from
Biblical times. The religious beliefs of the Children of Peace included
elements of both the Jewish and Christian faiths. Willson was an
impressive and convincing speaker and by 1840 his congregation
numbered some two hundred people. Music played an important
part in his services. ' ... from the galleries of the meeting house came
the music of a silver cornet band and the full-throated song of a
white robed choir.' Willson sometimes led processions of wagons to
Toronto with the choir and band. The accomplishments of the
Children of Peace in their first twenty years were impressive: a
meeting-house, day school, resident school for girls, mechanic shop
for boys, a music school, the first pipe organ in Upper Canada and,
their chief accomplishment, the Temple itself.

Phoebe Rogers, a travelling Quaker who passed through the village of Hope (Sharon) in 1821, writes in her diary, quoted in the
York Pioneer: 'These people have a great Meeting House; the inside
work, painting and organ altogether appear to show forth supersti-
tion and idolatry. David Willson gave us a sermon - it felt as if the
terrors of Death were in his doctrine! ... yet I believe there are many
tender hearts among them.'

William Lyon Mackenzie was impressed by the quality and diversity of the musical instruments. 'I had the curiosity to count their
instruments and there were three or four clarinets, two French horns,
two bassoons, besides German and Octave flutes, flageolets, etc.
They had also violins and violincellos, and are master of their delightful art.'

The organ, built in 1820, probably was the first actually constructed in Canada, as the usual procedure was to import organs

from England. The choir, too, was well known. Again William Lyon Mackenzie recalls: 'Early in the morning after I arrived, I found some of the singers in the chapel practising their hymns and tunes. A number of young females sang a hymn composed, as is all their poetry, by members of the society. Two young men had bass viols and the full-toned organ aided the music which, I will venture to say, is unequalled in any part of the Upper, and scarcely surpassed even by the Catholics in the Lower province.' The orchestra of the Children of Peace was probably the first Canadian band and by the mid-1860s was famous internationally as the Silver Band.

The Temple built by the Children of Peace remains today as does David Willson's study and the home of Ebenezer Doan, who was in charge of construction of the Temple. The house and study are in the Temple grounds and now in the care of the York Pioneer and Historical Society.

Sharon Temple: the gilded copper ball on high represents Peace

The Temple, built between the years 1825-30 on Lot 10, Concession 2, is unique in construction; it is symbolism in wood. It has been said that Willson gives the message through this building that, for lack of literary skill, he was unable to provide through writings.

If we begin with David Willson's vision, the building is self-explanatory. Willson saw his mission as the uniting of the Jewish and Christian faiths, the destroying of sectarianism and the beginning of the brotherhood of man. The Temple's square plan denotes unity and justice to all men. The Davidites would deal 'on the square' with all men. Three storeys represent the Trinity. Each side has a door - they are the four points of the compass, symbolizing the universality of faith and showing that people entered on an equal footing from every direction. Each side has an equal number of glass panes, that the light of the gospel might fall equally upon them all. Twelve lanterns and twelve columns represent the twelve Apostles. A gilded copper ball, suspended, represents Peace. Four central pil-

David Willson's study in the Temple grounds

lars represent faith, hope, love, and charity, and are linked by arches representing God's rainbow. A square altar houses the Ark, a miniature Temple containing the Bible.

The Temple was built, like Solomon's temple, in seven years, and the framework was prepared similarly - away from the holy site so it could be fitted together on the spot without disturbance from the voices of fools. The Ark, of inlaid walnut, was constructed without the use of nails. The white fence surrounding the Temple was the first of several zones of holiness through which a member passed to the holiest of all - the Bible in the Ark.

David Willson said the architectural plans came to him in a vision. Certainly it was a remarkable achievement to be able to direct this elaborate, ornate, and totally symbolic construction in 1825 when life was hard and even the essentials were hard to come by. Here in the bush, 30 miles north of York where no trails led east across the Township and pioneers had to hack their way through the

Ebenezer Doan house, Sharon Temple grounds

bush, the Children of Peace built a message in architecture. It is even more surprising that this Temple was not their regular meeting-house; in days of deprivation when luxuries were rare, here stood a Temple used only 15 times per year - once per month and for three special festivals, the most magnificent being the illumination in September when each of the 2952 panes of glass held a candle.

The Ebenezer Doan House is, as noted, also on the Temple grounds. It was moved there from the Doan farm on Yonge Street north of Sharon. Ebenezer Doan came from Pennsylvania in 1808 in a remarkable covered wagon which was constructed like a boat so that it would float across the streams. The poplar stick which he used to keep his cow moving during the trip was planted in the ground by his hand at the moment of arrival on his new land. It thrived, and subsequently switches taken from this stick have grown into poplar trees on the Queensville family farm. The Doan house, which was built in 1819, is a fine two-storey building of white frame,

The recessed door of 'Maplebyrn,' south of Sharon

attesting to the skill of the man who constructed the Temple. It is Georgian in style, with the sloping roof and small side chimneys so often found in early York County houses.

South of Sharon, on Lot 9, Concession 3W, is 'Maplebyrn,' the home of John T. Stokes, which was built in 1852. John Stokes was the architect and civil engineer who was responsible for Sir William Mulock's house on Yonge Street (see the chapter on Aurora) and the Presbyterian church in Newmarket. John Stokes was first a toll collector and then a tax collector; from this house he drove in his horse and buggy every day to his job as tax collector in Toronto. The present board-and-batten house was built around a smaller house already on the property. The door is unusual; it is deeply recessed with transoms in line with the inside of the wall. The jambs of the door-opening are panelled. The interior mouldings were hand-made by John Stokes. On one side of the house what appears to be a large window is actually a set of french doors. These, too, were hand-crafted by Stokes and are fitted with inside shutters that fold into decorative wooden pockets on each side. The board-and-batten shed was once a post office and attached to the house by a passage-way. The carving on the porch at the front is not original but was added later.

Another example of the outstanding work of John Stokes as architect is the Robert Brammer house on North Main Street, Sharon (Lot 11, Concession 3W), which was built for Brammer in 1857 using bricks from a nearby kiln. The columned porch which enclosed the house has been removed except for the back portion. It is thought that the front portico and pillars were a later addition. Brammer, a blacksmith, owned a mill in Sharon. The Brammer house is referred to as the 'doctor's house,' for evidence in the form of old bottles, pestles, and mortars has been found, indicating that at some time a doctor practised there. Scratched into the brick wall at the rear of the house are dates, recipes, and signatures of various occupants over the years. Some of these occupants must have spent uneasy nights, for descendants of the early owners recall tales of wolves roaming about the village, their eerie howling heard at night through the whole area. These stories were repeated by pioneers in the eastern portion of the township near Mount Albert, where also wolves haunted the farms.

'Walnut Farm,' on Lot 7, Concession 3W, just south of 'Maple-byrn,' was so named because Mrs Juda Lundy brought a black walnut with her from Albany, Illinois, when she came to live in East Gwillimbury. She planted the seed near the south-east corner of the present house, and the walnut tree still stands there today. The first building the Lundys built in 1830 was a log house; then in 1857 a builder constructed their white frame house from lumber that had been cut five years previously and had been lying by the road all that time to dry. The verandah has a curved roof, with slender posts, and, above it, three beautiful twelve-paned windows.

To the south of 'Walnut Farm' is a fine home built about 1845 by John Terry, whose father, an early settler, was active in politics. He was a member of the Reform group and took part in the Mackenzie Rebellion but escaped without being arrested. John met a violent fate nonetheless, for he died after being thrown from his sleigh when his horse bolted. At one time the house was surrounded on three sides by a verandah, part of which remains on one side. The house was originally built of square-cut logs, but has been cov-

Robert Brammer house, North Main Street, Sharon

ered with brick, now painted white.

The Terrys' neighbours to the south were the Samuel Haines family. They were Quakers from Pennsylvania who purchased Lot 4, Concession 2, in 1837 and no later than 1839 built a white frame house on the property. The original house that Samuel Haines built forms the back portion of the present dwelling, which has remained in the family; such continuing occupancy by the same family is common in rural York County but especially in East Gwillimbury. Tradition says that Samuel Haines exchanged a farm at Uxbridge (his other land holding) for a yoke of white oxen so that his wife could easily attend the meetings of the Children of Peace at Sharon and hear David Willson's fiery addresses.

On Lot 4, Concession 2W is the Brooks Howard house which dates from about 1850, confirmed by the fact that the present owners have found that the boards used in the frame are thicker than those which were produced post-1850 by machinery geared to

'Walnut Farm '

three-inch thickness. There is evidence of an old root cellar. The fine front door has a simple lintel and side lights. An unusual feature in the dining-room is the placement of four doors on one wall. This style is duplicated in the Peregrine house, on Lot 21, Concession 4W.

Another pioneer in East Gwillimbury, John Peregrine, arrived with his family from Staffordshire, England, in 1825 and spent his first four years in Upper Canada on a farm on Lake Simcoe where Mossington Park is now located. In 1829 he bought the farm on Lot 21, Concession 4W, on the present Don Mills Road, and built his house of stucco over frame. The land had been deeded to the Hollingshead family in 1803. Seven generations of Peregrines have lived on this farm. John's son David, a local preacher, celebrated his golden wedding in 1887 and was photographed in front of the house which, at that time, was enclosed by a verandah. David died two years later when he fell down the cellar stairs one night by mistaking the cellar door for that of his bedroom. The problem of having three doors in a row leaving the kitchen was presumably too much for an elderly man. The staircase has square posts and the original floors have wide planks.

'The Old Homestead' is the name of Wilmot Shepherd's log house built in 1834 on Lot 115, Concession 1E. Its simple plan suited the needs of the time – two rooms with a dormitory room above. At the back of the house, a storehouse was built of log and stone where fruits and vegetables were kept, but this has been replaced now with a shed.

The eastern portion of East Gwillimbury Township was settled later than the western, and with difficulty. Only an Indian bush trail led east from the settlement at Sharon when the first settlers, Samuel and Rufus Buchard, came in 1821. Rufus, Samuel, and Samuel's wife, Electa, came from Vermont and settled at what was later called Buchardtown. They endured enormous difficulties as did other settlers in the eastern part of the township as there were few rivers to support mills, and in order to get their grain ground they had to make a long walk to the western mills. In addition, wolves abounded and Electa Buchard was known to have used a tin horn to keep them at bay. In spite of these hardships and hazards, settlement did come slowly to the area and some characteristic early buildings can be seen today.

12

North Gwillimbury Township

The township of North Gwillimbury, like Gwillimbury East and West, was named for Major Gwillim, the father of Mrs Simcoe, wife of the first lieutenant-governor of Upper Canada. Since 1971 it has been part of Georgina Township, but this union was in fact a re-union, for the two townships were one until 1826, when North Gwillimbury became a separate entity. For the purposes of this book it seems convenient, however, to consider the township, once the smallest in York County, independently.

The village of Roches Point lies on the shore of Lake Simcoe at Cook's Bay. It was named after James Roche, who received a crown grant in 1808 for Lot 22, Concessions 2 and 3, the location of the present village. Much of this prominent point of land was subsequently bought by the government and the site was held for years as a possible alternative to York as the capital of Upper Canada. Although Simcoe had earlier moved the government offices from Niagara to York, Sir Peregrine Maitland, who was appointed lieutenant-governor in 1818, considered the Roches Point site to be superior. His wish to relocate the capital was based on two considerations: the site afforded complete protection from any possible harassment from the Americans, and he intended to develop the Trent and Rideau waterways as the main commercial and military routes - Roches Point was a link in the Yonge Street-Holland Landing-Trent River chain. The plan received no support, however, since officials and leading citizens, having suffered the move from Niagara to marshy York, were now well settled and most unwilling to renew pioneer life. A map of a government town plot, showing streets laid out, is in the York County historical atlas of 1878. The land was eventually sold.

Today four exceptional early buildings remain at Roches Point, three houses and one church, each unique. 'Lakehurst' was built about 1864 by Captain May, a British naval officer who commanded a steamship line which served parts of Lake Simcoe from a wharf located on his property. Captain May's house was not the first to be built on this property, for it had passed through the hands of a series of noteworthy owners. Timothy Rogers, whose part in the settlement of the Newmarket–Aurora area is of singular importance, owned the property until 1804; Rogers is frequently listed as holding early crown grants throughout East and North Gwillimbury, Whitchurch, and Vaughan townships. In addition, he was, as previously noted, responsible for leading groups of settlers to the York County area, supervising their initial efforts at settlement, and pass-

'Lakehurst,' Roches Point

ing on to them land he had held. Unlike many who obtained Crown grants, Rogers appears to have been interested primarily in procuring honest settlement, rather than in land speculation. In this instance, he sold the land to Calvin Eames, who, with his wife and sons and £500, had come to Upper Canada in 1802 after serving for six years in the Revolutionary army in Massachusetts. Calvin drowned in Cook's Bay in 1812 while on his way to grind his grain; his son, daughter-in-law, son-in-law, grandson, and an Indian guide perished with him. Eames had probably built a two-storey frame house in 1804. After his death, his wife and two surviving sons continued to live in it, and one of the sons, George Eames, worked the land.

In 1854 George Eames sold the property to W.B. Robinson, who sold it in 1859 to the Wyndham family. These owners must have added to and greatly enhanced George Eames's simple two-storey frame house, but the buildings were destroyed by fire and the land sold to

Fieldstone cabin, once a trading post, on 'Lakehurst' property

Captain May. Several buildings standing on the property today, however, represent the different periods of ownership. A fieldstone cabin which served as a trading post for the Indians is the oldest. An Eames descendant recalls tales of Indians camped around the post, challenging members of the family to wrestling matches. The nearby Georgina and Fox Island Indian reservations brought the business for the post.

Several board-and-batten outbuildings of the 1860 period surround Captain May's dignified Victorian Gothic house. Originally a frame structure, the house is now covered with stucco. Peaked windows and a trellised verandah look out on a magnificent expanse of property. On top of the house is a 'widow's walk,' a common feature of houses in Boston and the New England states, associated with a seafaring owner whose wife would look out from it to sea, watching for the return of her husband's ship, which, all too often, never came back.

Close to 'Lakehurst' is 'Beechcroft,' and on the same property, 'The Lodge.' The latter was once owned by Rev. Walter Stennett, who built Christ Church, Roches Point, and was rector there. Rev. Mr Stennett had first been a master at Upper Canada College, Toronto, and then, in 1857, principal. A nervous breakdown forced him to retire and he settled in Roches Point, where he had spent time at his parents' farm and had conducted services. For a while after his return he had to hold his services in Alfred Wyndham's barn, but in 1862 he designed and built Christ Church, Roches Point. A happy consequence of this activity was the complete recovery of his health. The church is of fieldstone and is built in the style of many English country churches.

Mr Stennett purchased the property on which both 'The Lodge' and 'Beechcroft' were built from Asa Crittendon in 1857. He in turn sold the property in 1870 to Anson G.P. Dodge and 'Beechcroft' was built by Dodge. Research into the history of 'Beechcroft' has provided a glimpse into the life of Dodge, an intriguing man. Little is known of him locally, but his name appears in an American historical novel, *The Beloved Invader*, by Eugenia Price. The author of the novel confirms that Dodge, who lived in New York City in the mid-19th century, and subsequently in the state of Georgia, left for Canada about 1870. After this his family lost touch with him. He belonged to a prominent American family and owned thriving lumber businesses in both the United States and Canada. The novel relates that he left his wife and son on several occasions, but his departure for Canada was the final break.

His firm, Dodge & Co., had extensive holdings in the Muskoka and Parry Sound areas of Ontario. The Orillia *Northern Light* reported in 1871 that 'The great lumbering firm of Dodge & Co. of New York employs more than 1000 Choppers here [Muskoka] and will put into American and Canadian marts more than 80 million feet of pine lumber the present year.' Anson Dodge was also president of the Georgian Bay Lumber Co., and vice-president of the Toronto, Simcoe, and Muskoka Junction Railway. It is not known where or when he died.

'Beechcroft' is gabled in front and surrounded by a verandah from which french doors open to all parts of the main floor. The light pouring through these doors gives to the interior a feeling of spaciousness and continuity with the outdoors. Recent renovations have exposed an early fireplace with pot-arm intact. 'Beechcroft'

Christ Church, Roches Point

has been in its time a school, a boarding-house, and a private residence. A present-day source recalls the time when it was a school for ministers. Numbers outside the rooms upstairs date from the boarding-house period. The thirty acres of 'Beechcroft' land were criss-crossed with a network of paths laid out for Dodge by Frederick Law Olmstead, the landscape artist who planned Mount Royal Park in Montreal and Central Park in New York.

'The Lodge,' of an earlier date than 'Beechcroft,' is built of fieldstone and is decorated with imaginative fretwork. Under a sloping roof, ornate mouldings broaden to a finely carved triangular base. The verandah roof is supported by peeled cedar poles and a round window looks out from beneath the peaked roof - a birdhouse effect which is repeated in the early bathing-house by the lake.

At the lower end of Cook's Bay, where North Gwillimbury begins, Concessions 1 and 2 are short because they lead directly to the lake. As a result they comprise only one or two lots. This cir-

'Beechcroft,' Roches Point

cumstance did not, however, deter the Department of Crown Lands from granting to John Goedike the crown deed for Lots 3 and 4 on Concession 1 in 1857 and charging him £80 for 200 acres of property. Goedike soon discovered that 'land' was an inexact description of what he had bought, and he employed a surveyor to confirm his findings. The surveyor's report, dated 1859, stated that the property granted was 'not land, not even swamp, but bog overgrown with wild rice.' The surveyor found that it was impossible to walk on the property in summer because it was 'highly dangerous, the surface is a floating mass of decayed vegetable matter.' In winter the walking was no better because 'numerous warm water streams made it dangerous to venture out,' even when Goedike's so-called land was frozen. During the following eleven years correspondence continued between Goedike and the Department of Crown Lands, as the owner of this non-land tried to recover his £80. In most respectful and restrained language, Goedike begged the honourable

'The Lodge,' Roches Point

gentlemen in the Department to consider his request and wondered politely why they did not care to answer his letters. Finally, just before the correspondence ended, the Department gave an answer: they would mark the matter 'for immediate attention.'

The records of early patentees in North Gwillimbury Township show a grant of land to Garrett Vanzante in 1803 for Concession 3, Lot 18. The deed reads 'located by Timothy Rogers.' Vanzante later acquired 200 acres of this property, and in 1803 he built the log house which stands virtually unchanged today. The property attached to the house has been reduced to fifty acres, and a frame addition was made to the rear in 1870. Repairs and constant care have, however, preserved this perfect example of an early Ontario log house, of the kind a settler would erect when ready to build something grander than a shanty. The Vanzante house is the 'improved' type, with partially squared logs. The interior was originally one room. Log houses were sometimes inclined to settle with age

Vanzante log house, Lot 18, Concession 3

and then separation of the logs might take place. The bottom log had to be placed on stones or given some other protection from the earth to prevent rot. In this house there are double logs at the bottom and the inner hardwood log still defies a drill. The original foundation, with a good cellar, remains.

Garrett Vanzante would have cleared the land, felling the trees in the season when there was little sap in them, removed the stumps, prepared the logs, and then called a house-erecting bee. After the framework was put up and the rafters in place, the rest - roofing, interior and exterior chinking and all interior trim - was left to the owner. Doors and windows were cut out by axe or saw after construction - a difficult task which ensured that windows were kept to a minimum. The Vanzante house, however, has more windows than the average log home. The cracks between the logs were filled with a mixture of chips, lime, mud, moss, and sand.

In 1807, Vanzante sold the house to Silas Eames, son of Calvin Eames who owned the 'Lakehurst' property. The prolific Eames family settled throughout the township. During the years that Silas Eames lived in the Vanzante cabin, he purchased property on which to settle his children. An 1809 census revealed that there were 73 persons living in North Gwillimbury; if all of Calvin's children were still in the township, they would have made up 30 per cent of the population. Silas Eames also participated in historic events; he was one of a company of men sent to Kingston with provisions in 1813 during the war with the United States; at Cobourg the company encountered the American fleet and were forced to turn back and march to York, 65 miles away.

A somewhat later log house, the property of Thomas Mossington, is located on Lake Concession 9, Lot 15, near Jackson's Point, then a 291-acre lot. The grant is dated 1836, and the house must have been built shortly thereafter. Thomas, son of the Georgina magistrate, built a refined version of the Vanzante type of house. The logs are well squared and fitted and are of substantial size. There have been changes: delicately carved mouldings, a verandah, and gables have been added. A recent major frame addition subtly blends the new with the old, even to the repetition of the porch mouldings.

The Mossington house probably would have possessed those amenities which were possible in log houses. These houses had floors of mud or rough logs. This one would have had sawn timber floors and possibly panelled walls. The living area would have included the fireplace with kitchen utensils near by and any accessories for spinning or weaving. The furniture would have been bought from a cabinet-maker or made by the owner (often of pine as it was the easiest wood with which to work).

A unique feature of the Mossington house was a trap-door in the floor which opened into a tunnel leading to Lake Simcoe (and a waiting boat), providing a fast exit in case of attack. Other protection was provided by guns strategically placed across the front of the house. A sundial on the lawn carries the inscription, 'Set me right and use me well and I ye Tyme to you will tell.'

Early maps of North Gwillimbury record hundreds of acres in Concessions 4, 5, 6, and 7 in the name of the Arnold family. This was the family of General Benedict Arnold, famed traitor to the American cause in the War of Independence, who was restored to the good graces of the British crown before his death in London. As a reward for his betrayal, Arnold and his family were granted

Mossington log house, near Jackson's Point

by the Surveyor-General of Canada, on October 29, 1799, 16,400 acres of land in North Gwillimbury Township. When Arnold died, his personal 5,000 acres were forfeited, but by his will, his widow, Margaret, in 1804 received 3,000 acres, and seven of his children 1,200 acres each. Two other sons, Richard and Henry, petitioned the Crown for land, but because they had received 2,000 acres each as subalterns, they were declared ineligible. Although the Arnold name is still listed on 1860 maps, there is no evidence that Margaret Arnold, her children, or their descendants, ever resided on any of the 11,400 acres; they probably held the land for many years and then sold it.

Land thus granted as a reward for services to the Crown did not advance the settlement of the area. The names of French nobility are also found in the early crown grants in North Gwillimbury, among them to Jean Louis, Vicomte de Chalus, in 1808, and to the Chevalier de Monseul in 1807. The Vicomte de Chalus received 500 acres in North Gwillimbury, but a much larger grant, 5000 acres 'including former grants, as a French loyalist, free of expense,' was to Quetton St George. As noted earlier, St George made his fortune eventually by trading, finding the life of a pioneer unsuitable, as did the other members of the French nobility. The township may have felt that these holdings conferred prestige, but certainly it did not benefit from either the presence or the labour of the owners.

From 1825 on, irregular covered-wagon stage services operated from Georgina Township to York. Travellers hauling grain or going to market often spent the night at the Belhaven Hotel, a stop on the stage route, Beaverton-Belhaven-Newmarket-York. Built by Mr Bovair and operated by Willy Culverwell, it eventually became known as the Culverwell Hotel. It burned down in 1895, but the hotel shed is still standing. The lower half of this two-storey building was used as a stable for the horses of guests. The upper half was multi-purpose, serving for council meetings, dances, Sunday School, auctions, and so on. On the lower level, the doors, each of a different design, recall the original use of the building as a stable, and a second-storey door opens to a hazardous drop to the ground.

In Belhaven, Lot 15, Concession 5, are the house and barns of Elemuel Draper. Names of members of the Draper family appear in lists of public offices from the first council meetings in 1822, occupying the positions of poundkeeper, fenceviewer, highway over-

seer, councillor, and finally reeve. Henry Draper was reeve in 1863
and 1866. Elemuel Draper, however, had a special claim to fame.
In his substantial barn he kept a team of flashy bay horses which
he drove out while sporting a 'plug' or 'stove-pipe' top hat and
white gloves. In this attire he met the coaches daily and so, in
Draper's honour, the village of Belhaven became known as 'Plug
Mount.' Elemuel was also one of the first men to own a cider mill
run by horsepower and a butter churn run by dogpower - neighbours brought their cream to him to be churned. The Draper house
is considerably older than the barn.

Near by is located the two-storey brick house of John Morton,
an imposing Georgian-style house: the simple balanced lines are
presented in early red brick produced in a local kiln. John Morton
was a descendant of the John Morton who was one of the 56 sign-
ers of the Declaration of Independence. The first schoolhouse in
the area was built on his property near where the present house

Bellhaven Hotel shed

stands. John Morton held various township offices, eventually becoming reeve in 1855, and again in 1862.

The two-storey plank house built by William Henry on Lot 16, Concession 6, has the distinction of being the largest of its type in York County. The house was built about 1858; since plank construction was usually used only for single-storey dwellings, this is a rare example of two storeys in plank. Pine boards three inches thick and two storeys high stand upright with no frame structure beneath, implanted in a plank four-sided rim at bottom and at top. The present owner, whose painstaking sanding and painting have restored the house, says that when cupboards were being added, the beams and planks were found to be absolutely level. These planks and beams, secured with wedges and fitted without the use of nails, have remained solidly in place since 1858. When the house was sold in 1865 to Ellis Sheppard, the land had been cleared and the barns were standing.

Elemuel Draper's barn, Bellhaven

At this time William Henry was reeve of North Gwillimbury. Both the Sheppard and Henry families have a long tradition of community service. The Sheppards were from Ireland, descendants of a Lord Mayor of Dublin. The Sheppard name is frequently attached to various township offices in the minutes of North Gwillimbury council meetings. These township minutes are particularly interesting because they reflect the problems of the times. Town meetings were strictly controlled and discipline was enforced. All persons holding property were required to do statute labour on the roads in order to maintain and improve them. The amount of labour was precisely defined but residents could petition to do labour in an area other than the one in which they resided. Wealthy landowners would not have done their statute labour personally, but would probably have paid someone to do it for them.

'Ainslie Hill,' Lot 21, Concession 7, on the Catering Road, is south-west of Sutton. The property was once held by the Canada

William Henry's plank house, largest of its kind in the county

Company. James O'Brien Bourchier, founder of Sutton, purchased the 200 acres in 1843 for the widowed mother of W.E.T. Corbett. The final documents, completed in 1847, mention buildings on the property, so it must be assumed that the present house and barns were completed before that time. 'Ainslie Hill' has been covered with stucco and the only trace of fieldstone is in a small smoke-house behind the main building. Deep windows look out on acres of wooded property and huge barns. Inside, fine old wood distinguishes an unusual double staircase: stairs at the front and the rear of the house meet in a central landing just below the second-floor level. In the barns the early windows remain, but those of the house have been replaced.

'Ainslie Hill' was sold in 1861 to James Anderson and his wife, the former Susanna Bourchier, James O'Brien Bourchier's daughter. Anderson came to North Gwillimbury after a career with the Hudson's Bay Company which had begun in 1831 at Moose Factory.

'Ainslie Hill,' south-west of Sutton

He was stationed at Lake Nipigon from 1846, and Fort Simpson from 1851 to 1857; in 1854 he was Chief Factor; and in 1855 he headed the Anderson-Stuart expedition in search of Sir John Franklin. The Anderson family was indeed adventurous. The explorations of James's brother, A.C. Anderson, are important in the history of British Columbia. He spoke the Indian tongues and the French of the fur traders and his journals record scaling precipices and shooting rapids in search of routes to the coast.

In 1949 'Ainslie Hill' passed out of the hands of the Anderson family when it was sold to Irving Robertson, son of John Ross Robertson of the Toronto *Telegram*.

13

Georgina Township

Stephen Leacock, one of Georgina's most famous sons, said of the early development of the township, 'It seems strange to think that so recently as the days of the American Revolution, when Boston was already an old town and Montreal had a century and a half behind it, the Lake Simcoe Country lay empty and uncultivated.' Settlement did come slowly, partly because of the difficulty of transportation to Georgina, for the journey up Yonge Street to Holland Landing was only the initial stage in a trip which included a voyage across Lake Simcoe's unpredictable waters. The first steamboat to serve the lake was built at Holland Landing in 1832, and the shareholders included Thomas Mossington, Major W. Raines, J.O. Bourchier, J.M. Jackson, and Samuel Lount. The service prospered and other ships were added, including the *Enterprise*, after which Stephen Leacock's famous 'Mariposa Belle,' of *Sunshine Sketches of a Little Town*, was patterned. By 1842, however, there were still only 586 residents in Georgina Township.

The social development of Georgina was rather different from that of other townships in York County. Sutton and Pefferlaw sprang up quickly because one man almost singlehandedly established each village, James O'Brien Bourchier at Sutton and Captain William Johnson at Pefferlaw. A second stage in the development of Georgina is represented by the gracious houses still located on the shores of Lake Simcoe. They were built by highly educated, cosmopolitan immigrants, members of the British upper class.

Georgina was named in honour of George III in the time of Lieutenant-Governor Simcoe, but settlement did not begin until 1819, when Captain William Bourchier and his brother James acquired land there. During the War of 1812, when the naval forces of the United States controlled the Upper Lakes, Captain Bourchier had been involved in planning the construction at Penetanguishene of a battleship of which he was to have had command. During this operation an anchor was hauled from York to Holland Landing by 50 yoke of oxen - an event long recalled by pioneers. After the war, Bourchier was granted 2000 acres of land, of which he deeded 700 acres to his brother. William married Amelia Jackson, daughter of John Mills Jackson, after whom Jackson's Point on Lake Simcoe was named, and the couple left for India. James remained and he and John Comer were Georgina's first settlers.

Bourchier built a sawmill on the Black River at Sutton, a grist mill dating 1819, which was rebuilt in the 1830s, and a general store. The mill, one of the first buildings erected in Georgina, still stands in its picturesque setting. The original red stain can be seen on the exterior at the back. The appearance of the front is, however, greatly altered. An attractive feature of the building is its well-proportioned windows.

Private mills such as Bourchier's were essential to a new community. Home milling was extremely difficult, the grain being usually put into a hollow stump or similar device and crushed with stones, an axe, or sometimes a cannonball. Since long trips by sleigh or canoe to a grist mill were the alternative, and mills provided by the government were few, a local private mill soon found customers and was usually followed by settlement around it. Later on, some of the millers took advantage of the situation and began to overcharge. Since it was customary for the miller to keep part of the ground wheat as toll or payment, Lieutenant-Governor Simcoe put through an act forbidding millers to take more than one-twelfth of the grist in payment. A distillery was usually soon attached to a grist mill so that poorer quality or surplus grain could be turned into whiskey. Since this product was also in great demand, breweries and distilleries were as common as grist and saw mills.

The Bourchier store, of board-and-batten construction, backed on to the river, where the river door once opened to Indian traders and other river travellers. Solidly built, the cellar walls are three feet thick and the hand-made nails and hardware can still be seen. As with the mill, its appearance from Main Street gives little clue to its early date.

James O'Brien Bourchier was a leading citizen in the community, becoming Justice of the Peace in 1829. He owned the sawmill, gristmill, woollen mill, manor house, and cheese factory. He also was post-master. By 1837, he was actively supporting the government against the rebels, as was to be expected in a man of his background. The aristocratic Bourchier family traced its lineage back to John Bourchier, who was created Earl of Essex by Edward III in 1342. Subsequently the family tree had included a granddaughter of Edward III, an Archbishop of Canterbury, a captain of the King's Horse Guard of Henry VIII, and other distinguished Englishmen.

By 1842, the first schoolhouse was built in Sutton. It also served as the first church and town meeting hall. It is located on River Street and its simple uncluttered lines give it timeless appeal.

In 1845 James Bourchier built his second home, the 'Manor,' which is still one of the finest pioneer homes in the township. Built

Bourchier's Mill, Sutton

of brick, its symmetrical facade is surrounded by a low graceful verandah. Joan Martyn describes it thus in an unpublished thesis for the Faculty of Architecture, University of Toronto: 'Its carriage house and stable, its barn, smoke house, henhouse and gardens were built in loyalist Georgian style - the only style at the time for the town's most important citizen ... An obvious centre hall plan, it has a large kitchen wing projecting from the back and a summer kitchen beyond that. The room behind the front living room on the right was a schoolroom for the Bourchier children. Two Leacock girls also attended. Over the kitchen, the cupola had a large bell specially cast in England in 1845 and serving until recently as a town clock.'

The Sutton Town Hall, although altered, dates back to the early 1850s when it was built by Bourchier as a woollen mill. Since that time it has served as a cheese factory, jail, marketplace, post office, barber shop, and library.

St James Anglican Church in Sutton was built in 1857 through

River Street School, Sutton

The cupola over the kitchen of the 'Manor'

The 'Manor,' Main Street, Sutton, built by James Bourchier in 1845

the generosity of Bourchier's English relatives. It followed a Gothic design. At the urging of his wife, Bourchier then donated the land on which the Presbyterian Church was built. This church was not completed until 1866 and is still standing as part of the new Knox United Church. James O'Brien Bourchier died in 1872. As a tribute to him, the flag on top of St Lawrence Hall in Toronto was lowered at his death.

Two other pioneer homes in Sutton bear mentioning. 'Maplehurst,' built in 1850 on River Street, derived its name from an immense maple tree which once stood beside it. The other house, built by Thomas Wheatley in 1850, is located on the north side of High Street at the east end of Sutton. Today this fine old board-and-batten building shows the result of a diligent restoration program. The house originally consisted of two storeys containing six rooms. A front and side porch were added in the 1920s and a further addition was made during recent restoration. The house was not

St James Church, Sutton

built on this site but was moved to it from a neighbouring township when purchased by Margaret and Isabella Howard in 1902. The house is now called the Eames house after the family which bought it in the 1920s and lived in it until recently.

After the battle of Waterloo, Captain William Johnson, R.N., retired and settled in 1819 in the eastern part of Georgina Township. Like Bourchier in Sutton, Johnson founded a village, which he called Pefferlaw. In 1832, with the help of his brother Robert, who had emigrated from Scotland, he built the first Pefferlaw store and post office. On other parts of his 1000-acre grant, he erected a sawmill, woollen mill, and grist mill. On the main street of Pefferlaw stands the Union Hotel built in 1857. The lower part has been altered so that much of the original flavour of the building has been lost.

Captain Johnson was a friend and supporter of William Lyon Mackenzie, although he preferred constitutional methods of reform

'Maplehurst,' River Street, Sutton

to violent ones. His home was open to Mackenzie, who frequently spent time there. This connection was the cause of Johnson's alienation from other prominent families who, as English immigrants, remained firm supporters of the Family Compact. Captain Johnson, therefore, was at odds with such families as the Sibbalds and Mossingtons, mentioned later in this chapter.

Johnson's diary, as published in *Georgina*, by Paget Hett, recalls the feelings of the times:

May 5*th*, 1837 – Received a letter from the Lieut.-Governor thanking me for my explanation of the charges made against me by the four informing Tory Commissioners, Arad Smalley, Francis Osborne, J.O. Bourchier and Henry Stennet exculpating me from any blame.

December 27*th* – Went to Toronto to answer the charge of High Treason.

December 18*th*, 1844 – Mr. MacKenzie came last night to see me!

December 25*th*, 1848 – Eleven years ago I was arrested by the Black Orangemen and carried before the Commissioners at Toronto for High Treason, without any summons except their pistols ... I am pleased beyond measure that we can now sit down in safety under a benign and responsible government.

A wave of settlement which had no counterpart in York Country took place in the 1830s on the shores of Lake Simcoe. Several prominent families emigrated from England to Canada and established country estates on the lakeshore. These were vast properties for the time, with manor houses, barns, stables, and workers' lodgings, all set in what was then rugged country.

Major William K. Raines, a veteran of the Peninsular War, boasted the title, 'Knight of the Grand Cross of the Order of Leopold,' granted by Emperor Francis I of Austria. In the 1820s he built 'Penn Raines' or 'Penn Range,' with the idea of founding a colony. It was also called 'Sutton Lodge,' hence the town's name. In 1835, however, he moved on and sold his home to Mrs Susan Sibbald. It now forms part of 'Eildon Hall' in Sibbald Provincial Park, and is open to the public during the summer months. Little is known of Major Raines, but he was described as 'a jovial gentleman, notorious for his success with the fair sex.' It is said that when he left 'Penn Raines,' he was accompanied by two beautiful sisters whom he had met while crossing the Atlantic and had persuaded to live with him and share his affections.

Mrs Susan Sibbald came to Canada first through her concern for two of her sons who she had learned were living in a tavern in Orillia. The sons, William and Charles, had been sent to Canada in 1833 to learn farming. Colonel Sibbald's decision to send his sons overseas had been made on the advice of his friend Sir John Colborne, then Lieutenant-Governor of Upper Canada. In the adventurous spirit of some British ladies of the period, Susan Sibbald undertook this lengthy journey to determine whether her sons were leading moral lives or had fallen into wicked ways in the colonies. After satisfying herself that her offspring had remained virtuous, she toured the area. Charmed by 'Penn Raines,' which she subsequently renamed 'Eildon Hall' after her childhood home in Scotland, she purchased it along with its 500-acre farm. She moved into her new home in 1835. Paget Hett, in *Georgina*, tells of her life there:

For nearly three months in the depth of winter, Mrs Sibbald lived in Eildon

'Eildon Hall,' Sibbald Provincial Park

Hall, sparsely furnished and uncomfortable, and her mind much disturbed by anxiety about her husband's health, by the fact that a tavern stood on her property, and that there was no church in the neighbourhood.

When she left for Scotland with her son Archibald on March 1, 1836, she had arranged for the removal of the tavern and had promised her support to the building of a church.

On returning to Scotland, Mrs Sibbald discovered that her ailing husband had died during her absence, so she settled her affairs and returned with the rest of the family and all their treasured possessions. This was no mean feat considering that it meant transporting large pieces of furniture, oil paintings, and valuable china and books over the high seas, up pioneer roads, and across Lake Simcoe by steamer.

Susan Sibbald made many improvements to the property and to the house. Stephen Leacock says in his article, 'The Lake Simcoe Country': 'Most notable of all these southern settlements is Eildon Hall, the family home of the Sibbalds, dating back to a log house built in the 1820's and in point of beauty unsurpassed.'

During the years 1835-43, old world customs were maintained at 'Eildon Hall.' The Sibbalds had a full stable of horses and exotic gardens. While farm chores consumed a large part of the working day, the family still found it possible to continue certain customs associated with the gracious life they had led in Scotland. Sibbald diaries record the way in which the difficulties of maintaining a good working farm were balanced by the pleasures to which the family was accustomed:

Tom, Mr Ritchie and myself had a grand concert in the afternoon ...
Miss Turner and Miss Isabella spent the afternoon with croquet and other amusements ...
Cleaned out the pond. Underbrushed near the Boat House ...
Took a pull in the boat before tea ...

Susan Sibbald later moved to Toronto where she died in her eighties, having numbered among her friends members of Toronto's prominent families: Sir John Beverley Robinson, Bishop Strachan, and others.

William Bourchier returned from India in 1837 after the death of his wife. He built near Jackson's Point a magnificent home, 'The Briars,' which is said to have been named after Napoleon's temporary residence before he was sent to St Helena (this residence was the home of William Balcombe of the East India Company, a close friend of Bourchier's). 'The Briars' was sold to Frank Sibbald in the 1870s. Sibbald added the wings, built a coach-house, and constructed a fanciful octagonal peacock house for his imported peacocks. Frank's diaries tell of the work:

1877 – Drove to Sutton in the afternoon. Arranging for purchase of the Briars ... Pulling out stumps south of the barn ... In a great mess with painters and carpenters ... Seeded the fallow to south of the house ... From the Briars to Eildon Hall in less than one hour ... Three carpenters working putting up pig pens ... Received discharge on mortgage on the Briars property from William Bourchier ...

Today the coach-house, main house, and unique peacock house remain, still in good condition.

'The Briars,' east of Jackson's Point

The frame and stucco house built by Thomas Mossington on the Lake Shore Road, east of the Black River, is called 'Plumstead,' after Mossington's home in England. Mossington was sent to Canada in 1808 by the British Admiralty to locate timber for the masts of the British Navy and remained for two years. On his retirement from the navy he returned to Canada, in 1830, and became a successful magistrate in Georgina. He was renowned for his fair decisions in the many eruptions that occurred in pioneer life. The dining-room at 'Plumstead' served as his courtroom while another part of the house doubled as a school.

Mossington was the master builder and foreman in the erection of the first St George's Church built in 1838 near what is now Sibbald Memorial Park. He prepared the plans and personally made a wooden model of the building. On 25 May 1838, construction began and William Sibbald's diary records: 'Mr Mossington came to the church grounds to lay out the site for the church. Mr Bourchier

Peacock house at 'The Briars'

brought down a raft of 15,000 feet of timber.'

In 1841 Thomas Mossington married a 21-year-old girl and the occasion was marked by a 'Shivaree.' This had become the custom when a second marriage occurred soon after the death of the former partner, or when there was a considerable age disparity between bride and groom, as in this case. John Sibbald describes Thomas Mossington's Shivaree (quoted in *Georgina*):

January 5th, 1841 – Mr Mossington, one of our neighbours, an old gentleman with a numerous family, married a Miss Donnell, aged 21. The people at Sutton and Bourchiers Mills concluded that they would give him a Shivaree – a Canadian custom. All the idlers, loafers and blackguards about a Township repair to the newly married couple's house at night and serenade them with sleigh bells, cow bells, and every other noisy article they can get hold of and shout and make a row until the persecuted husband bribes them to go away by giving them some liquor. About forty of them, boys and men, headed they

Coach house, 'The Briars'

say by Mr Corbett late of H.M. 60th Regiment, in a female dress, assembled at 10 p.m. at old Mossington's and kicked up an infernal row enough to wake the seven sleepers. Old Mossington, who does everything methodically, came and tried to identify the parties in case they might do any harm. He told them he would give them an order on the Tavern at the Mill for a gallon of whiskey if they would go away. They complied at first, but after pocketing the order, they said they must drink his health there, so that he was obliged to fork out four bottles more before they would depart in peace.

Captain Simon Lee was also a pioneer of some position. He had recently retired from the East India Company when he settled near the Sibbalds in 1836 on the lake immediately east of what is now Sibbald Park, after living for some time on Yonge Street (as described in the chapter on Thornhill). Captain Lee settled at the eastern limit of the Sibbalds' property on 500 acres of land and built the two-storey frame house, 'Lee Farm' which still stands to-

'Lee Farm,' east of Sibbald Park

day. A large verandah has been removed and new siding added, but the Lee home still has the original pine floor, 24-paned sashes, and the first glass with its tell-tale bubbles. The Lees had three daughters, who married William Sibbald, Captain Stupart, and John Barwick respectively. William Sibbald had first chosen the second daughter, who was later to become Mrs Stupart, but her mother announced that the three girls must be taken in order of age. Emily, being the eldest, was slated for the oldest suitor, William Sibbald. Although William initially agreed, the only way he could be persuaded to the altar when the wedding day came was with the aid of a liberal portion of brandy. The marriage, however, turned out to be an exceedingly happy one.

The original St George's Church was built in 1838 because of a determined plea for a house of worship by the Sibbalds, Jacksons, Mossingtons, and other residents. The church was erected on land given by Susan Sibbald and John Comer. The long struggle for permission to build the church was headed by John Mills Jackson. For reasons now difficult to understand, the Anglican church hierarchy was slow to respond to the wishes of the would-be parishioners. Jackson had come to Canada in 1806 without the intention of settling, but had made an instant resolve to return as soon as he could settle his affairs in England. Before he came back he caused a stir at home with his pamphlet, *A View of the Political Situation of the Province*, for he attacked the system of Clergy Reserves. Returning to Georgina to live, he initiated the church project and pursued it to the end, in spite of the loss of his eyesight. The Anglican church donated the munificent sum of £25, and in the end the building was financed locally without any other help from official church bodies. The Bishop of Quebec refused any assistance, even to a fund for a temporary frame schoolhouse to be used as a church. Lieutenant-Governor Simcoe was a contributor, however, and his seven daughters painted and donated the east window. Hugh Sibbald wrote, 'I was welcomed by Mrs Simcoe and the daughters took me to a workshop. They are now engaged in making a painted window for our church.'

In 1876 the early church was demolished and the present stone building erected in its place in memory of Susan Sibbald. One memorable character who took part in its construction was Captain Thomas Sibbald. He introduced naval practices on the job site, appearing each day at 'eight bells' to issue the rum ration and supervise the toasting of the Queen's health. His remarks were replied to by the men with 'Aye, aye, sir.' His self-appointed task was to supervise the stone-cutting to ensure that no iron could be seen in any of the stones used. Only one stone escaped his notice, and it can be seen today showing the rusty stain. St George's cemetery is the burial place of Stephen Leacock and of Mazo de la Roche, as well as of many members of the Sibbald family.

Inland, on Concession 6, Lot 4, stands one of the few stone houses in Georgina. It was built in 1840 by the first reeve of Georgina, Charles Howard. Howard came to Canada in 1819, where he lived first at Port Hope and then moved to Georgina. The house was named 'St Julian's.'

While the Bourchier mill, described earlier in this chapter, was serving those settlers who located in the area which is now Sutton, another mill was operating on the Black River from the early 1800s in the town of Baldwin to the south. The gristmill standing in that

St George's Church

Baldwin Mill on the Black River

town today is the third to occupy the site as the two previously located in Baldwin were destroyed by fire. Built in Keswick in 1879, the present mill was moved to Baldwin when it was purchased by William Heise. It had a 65-acre mill pond, and three turbines which are still operational. The Baldwin mill was in full production as recently as 1968. The structure is perfectly functional but in addition its symmetry of line has been a constant attraction for artists who, in interpreting the mill and its source of power, the Black River, have exemplified the fact that the nucleus of the early pioneer community was also an aesthetic attraction.

14

Scarborough

Although Scarborough is now predominately an urban borough, it still shows evidence of its earlier existence as an agricultural township composed of small unincorporated villages. First settled in 1796, Scarborough developed slowly in some areas because much of the land was divided into large farms and that which was not under cultivation was held for speculation and hence was unavailable for purchase.

Because of the present density of population and prevalence of high-rise buildings, it takes detective work to find pioneer Scarborough. The strongest impression upon locating the remaining buildings of the early 19th century is of the striking beauty of the fieldstone so skilfully worked by Scottish stonemasons. In each township, pioneer builders used the material which was most readily available. In North York the good clay lent itself to the moulding of mud or baked brick, and we have brick houses. In areas such as Thornhill, where many sawmills were operating, frame buildings predominate. In Scarborough stones, heavy in weight and of various shadings and colours, were to be found in the fields and rivers. The old stone buildings now standing on main traffic arteries must have been built with stone from the fields, while those near the alternative artery, the Rouge River, would have used stones taken from the river bed.

For a long time Scarborough was a Scottish community. The Scottish pioneers introduced curling to the area and it became a popular winter sport. For this reason, much of the fallow land was planted with Scottish broom heather so that it could be used in the making of curling brooms. The Scottish game of draughts was another import and became known as checkers. The township abounded with checker players, including William Fleming who was undefeated in twenty years of play throughout many parts of Upper Canada.

David Thompson, a Scottish stonemason from Dumfriesshire, had settled in York in 1796 and helped to erect the government buildings there. He decided to move to the country because of the illness caused by the dampness around the bay at York; he wished to establish his homestead on well-drained rich earth which would support a farm. It is also related that his wife Mary insisted upon the move and continued insisting until it was accomplished. When Thompson first made the journey to Scarborough to locate land, he had to hike twelve miles along an Indian trail which led from the small settlement on the bay at York, and three miles further into untouched forest. Here he located his farm on Lot 24, Concession 1, and, soon after clearing some land, built an oak and pine log house. This was the first land cleared in Scarborough. The property was near the present site of St Andrew's Church in Thompson Park.

During the following winter, Thompson was obliged to spend long periods in York completing his work on the government buildings. This left Mary alone in their house in the forest with five children, no neighbours, and the Canadian winter to contend with as well as the varied chores of caring for home and animals. It is said that when she once saw a bear attacking one of their few pigs she picked up the axe and, running at the bear, struck it full force. However, the dangers from wild animals and the difficulties of a pioneer existence were compensated for by the friendliness of the Indians in the area; trade with them was carried on at the kitchen door.

It was not until the Danforth Road was built at the turn of the century, 1799-1800, that David Thompson could go from his property to York without walking the fifteen miles. In 1815, he erected a large frame house (no longer standing) to accommodate his family in relative comfort. He died in 1834, having just endured, without benefit of anaesthetic, the amputation of one leg which had gangrened. His life's savings were distributed to his ten sons and daughters, £22 to each.

Shortly after David and Mary Thompson's arrival in Scarborough, David's brothers, Andrew and Archibald, stonemason and carpenter respectively, arrived with their families. They found David already the possessor of 600 acres of land - the original 400-acre grant and 200 extra acres given 'in consideration of the Petitioner's [Thompson's] large family and his being the first settler who has built a house and resides in Scarborough.' Andrew and Archibald Thompson probably are responsible for most of the fieldstone houses in the area, for they not only built many of them themselves but were instrumental in establishing the Scottish tradition of craft apprenticeship. Archibald had served under the Mohawk chief, Joseph Brant, during the American Revolution, and was commissioned as lieutenant in the York militia; he later became a Justice of the Peace and a leading citizen of Scarborough.

Thompson Memorial Park was created to honour the memory of the Thompsons, Scarborough's first settlers. Although the original log and frame houses built by David Thompson no longer exist, the church founded by the Thompsons is still standing and near by are two early Thompson houses, those of David's nephew James and son William.

St Andrew's Presbyterian Church in Thompson Park was built in 1849 to replace an earlier wooden building erected on land donated by James Thompson. A simple brick structure, its unpretentious design reflects the character of the early Scottish settlers who worshipped there. In the adjacent cemetery, both David and Mary Thompson are buried along with many other settlers. To this first church many hardy Scotsmen trudged six miles to sit on wooden benches and partake of a service which lasted for five hours and included a sermon of one and one-half hours' length.

The first school in Scarborough was built in 1817 on the Thompson farm. Even before this, however, one of the first circulating libraries in Canada had started from David and Mary Thompson's personal collection of books. The collection was housed in a frame building erected in 1846. The present library, beside St Andrew's church, was constructed as part of Scarborough's centennial celebration in 1896, which commemorated one hundred years of settlement.

A short distance to the east of the church, at 146 St Andrew's Road, is the home of James Thompson. Known as 'Springfield Farm,' this large house was built in 1840 on the side of a hill, with two storeys at the front and one at the back - a 19th-century split-level. The house is of red brick on a stone foundation and its symmetrical design is enhanced by a simple wooden verandah which graces it on two sides. A root house adjacent to the main house remains. It is said that the workers building St Andrew's Church in 1849 boarded here while the church was being completed.

West of 'Springfield Farm,' at the corner of Brimley Road and St Andrew's Road, is another Thompson house, that of William, David's son; it was called 'Bonese,' after the old family home in Westerkirk, Scotland. 'Bonese' is a substantial fieldstone house with a barn-style roof and, until recently, was occupied by the great-granddaughter of David and Mary. The present house differs somewhat from the original; during the 1920s the roof was removed and another storey added. This addition explains the presence of dormers, which are not typical of the earlier period.

In Thompson Park stands the home of another early resident, Fred S. Cornell, descendant of a pioneer, William Cornell. The Cornell family came to Scarborough just after the Thompsons. William

St Andrew's Church, Thompson Memorial Park

built a log house on Markham Road and a mill on Highland Creek in 1799. To obtain the millstones, he went to Kingston by sleigh, paid for the stones by giving colts in exchange, and pulled the stones back to Scarborough by sleigh. When Cornell and his neighbour, Levi Annis, found that they were poorly served by the Danforth Road, they cut their own road out of the bush - at first only a trail - and called it 'Cornell' or 'Front' road. The Cornell house in the park was built in 1850 by Isaac Stoner and was originally located on the Markham Road in what was called Scarborough village. Fred Cornell and his sister Tillie lived in this simple frame building which now serves as a museum under the care of the Scarborough Historical Society.

Beside the Cornell house is a settler's cabin, circa 1833. It was built and first owned by Mark Hutchinson, but in 1848 was bought by W.P. McCowan and remained in the McCowan family for over one hundred years. The present McCowan Road is named after

'Springfield Farm,' 146 St Andrew's Road

Willie McCowan. Originally located on Lot 13, Concession 4, the cabin was moved to the park and restored to the condition in which it existed in 1940, at which time in its long history the dormer windows were added.

Upon hearing of the successful settlement of his aunt, Mary Thompson, Archibald Glendinning emigrated from Scotland in 1820 and bought 200 acres of land at Ellesmere and Kennedy Road in what was later called the village of Ellesmere. In ten years he had prospered so well that he could build a large stone house using stones gathered from the land. At one time Archibald Glendinning operated the post office and one of the first stores in the township from the large front room of his house.

One of the finest houses in Scarborough is the Thomas Glendinning house located on Pharmacy Avenue, south of Steeles - a beautiful example of Upper Canadian Gothic revival. Painted brickwork gives the lacy effect of Victorian 'gingerbread' to the gable. Amid

'Bonese,' Brimley and St Andrew's Roads

its present surroundings, the appearance of this mid-19th century architecture is startling. The date 1870 is in the glass above the door.

The lasting results of the work of Scarborough's pioneer stone-masons can be seen throughout the borough. The early home built by Timothy Devenish for his father William, at 1355 Victoria Park Avenue, combines stone with interesting brickwork at the corners and over the windows, together with a brick driveway. The choice of fieldstone as a building material was not only practical, because the stones had to be moved in order to cultivate the land, but aesthetic, as can be seen in the timeless beauty of the stones in the houses remaining today. The Devenish family first came to Canada in the 1790s and William and his wife settled on a farm near the present St Clair Avenue in Scarborough. The isolation of their location was such that, in desperate anxiety to have a neighbour, they gave a life-lease on 100 acres of their land for one shilling a year. Even this effort was short-lived as the tenant died, and his widow

Cornell house and McCowan log cabin, Thompson Memorial Park

was tragically murdered during an unsuccessful attempt to find the savings which were sewn safely into her mattress.

On Markham Road, just south of Sheppard Avenue, is a superb work in stone, the 1857 house of William Purdy. The date is carved over the door and the simplicity of the Upper Canadian cottage style is enhanced by the selection of stones and skill of workmanship. The traditional door, with lights and two twelve-paned windows, is set off by the colour and texture of the materials.

Three other stone houses in the area are of importance. The A. Stirling house at Finch and Neilson was built in 1860 and maintains the original interior. It is soon to be a Scarborough Historical Society office. The Thomas Jacques house at Staines Road and Finch Avenue dates from about 1850. Jacques was a noted rival of William Fleming as champion checker player. The Scott house built in 1841 is located just south of McCowan Road and Highway 401. It is a

Thomas Glendinning house, Pharmacy Avenue

fine two-storey building at present facing the plaza of Scarborough Town Centre.

The house built for the rector of St Margaret's Church in the late 1830s still stands on the north bank high above the valley on Scarborough Golf Club Road. This is a delightful house which has been well cared for duirng the years. Only slightly altered, it still exhibits many features of early Upper Canadian style such as fine windows and double chimneys. This house was built for and occupied in 1840 by Rev. William Henry Norris when he emigrated from England with his bride to become rector of St Margaret's. In 1856 Norris also became a Justice of the Peace for York County. In addition, he was instrumental in organizing the militia and was active during the Fenian raids, at which time he became a lieutenant-colonel.

One of the oldest buildings in Ontario is the log cabin at the Guild Inn, which was built in 1796. There are two theories concern-

Devenish house, 1355 Victoria Park Avenue

ing its construction. The first is that the cabin was built by William Osternaut to whom the crown grant was given in 1799. Osternaut, originally from the Netherlands, moved to Niagara in 1786 and to Scarborough in 1796. The other theory names Augustus Jones, original surveyor of the area, as the builder. He was said to have built it as a shelter for his crew as they went up and down the lake carrying out his first survey. The log cabin has been occupied almost continuously since it was built on this location and at present is a home for Canadian authors and artists. The property was once owned by Alexander Macdonnell, Speaker of the House of Assembly in 1804, and afterwards by Duncan Cameron, Provincial Secretary and Registrar of Upper Canada.

John Pearse, another of Scarborough's earliest settlers, was a Yorkshire yeoman, a landowner and farmer, and the large fieldstone residence, carriage-house, and barn built for him on Reesor Road show his good sense in using the excellent materials at hand. This com-

Scott house, near Highway 401 and McCowan Road

plex is unique and probably the most beautiful in the area. All three buildings were erected in 1852 and only the barn no longer exists. The creek near by, a branch of the Rouge River, supplied the stone for the full two-storey house, for the barn, and for what must be one of the very few carriage-houses in Ontario equal in size to the house and also containing a separate second storey. Pearse used slate for his roof, the walk in front of the house, and a path overlooking the river. Unfortunately the slate, which was shipped from England, was unable to withstand the rigour of Canadian winters, but there remains some evidence of it. The windows in both house and carriage-house are deeply recessed and set off by lovely old twelve-paned sashes. The bake-oven and fireplace remain in the basement. The same standards of construction were applied to the carriage-house as to the main house and equal attention paid to details of design.

At one point in the history of the Pearse house it was bought by

Pearse house, Reesor Road

George McTavish. The previous owner, deciding after the sale that he had let the house go too cheaply, broke into the building one night and chopped up the pine floor in the dining-room to even matters. Subsequently the mangled pine was replaced with maple, but this is the only hardwood floor in the house. This property has been set aside as green belt by the government and its tenure appears to be secure.

On Lot 9, Concession 4, is the original home of William Milne. He had built a mill on the west side of the Rouge River and wanted a river site for his house. The ruins of the gristmill still remain and the sluice of the mill-pond can be seen; however, the pond itself was destroyed during the flooding which occurred during Hurricane Hazel in 1955. The ice-house, with the date 1870 carved in the wall, is still on the property. The house is constructed of white pine with vertical siding in board-and-batten style. Additions have been made at intervals, including the elaborate gingerbread and the dormer

Pearse's carriage house, built in 1852

windows. An intricately worked wood fence and a grove of 70-year-old walnut trees enclose the property. The Milne family sided with William Lyon Mackenzie during the Rebellion and, in order to escape from the militia which pursued them subsequently, are said to have sought safety in their own root-cellar and so remained undetected.

Another early and outstanding house is located on Brimley Road just north of Finch. Marshall Macklin, a young Irish immigrant, bought 200 acres of heavily wooded land here from the Canada Company in 1827 and shortly thereafter erected a log cabin. The cabin now forms the rear portion of the house and is used as a kitchen and study. The Macklin family grew rapidly to include seventeen children, and the present stone house, called 'Forest Home,' was built to accommodate them. The interior of the building indicates the care with which the Macklins planned. The rooms are well proportioned and generous in size and pine from the property was used

William Milne house, on the west side of the Rouge River

Milne house

throughout for floors and woodwork. The basement is of fieldstone
with a mud floor. Descendants of the Marshall Macklins occupied
the house for many years, maintaining it in fine condition and preserving the original furniture, farm and kitchen utensils, and china.

A most important early name in Scarborough was Annis. Charles
Annis, born in Enniskillen, Ireland, in 1638, emigrated to the American colonies in 1662. His descendant, Charles, came to Upper Canada in 1781 to investigate the land for settlement and came to settle
in the Oshawa area in 1793. It is reported that when crossing the
border, Annis was asked if he had supported King George in the
American uprising. He replied that he always would support the
country that was his home, and its people. This answer is said to
have impressed Governor Simcoe immensely. Journeying east,
Charles found some magnificent wooded land on the Scarborough
Bluffs and left two sons there while he went farther on. It is reported of Charles Annis that, at one point, he turned down an offer
to trade a two-year-old heifer for the 100 acres on which Eatons'
main store in Toronto now stands.

Levi Annis, son of Charles, and his wife Rhoda (daughter of
Roger Conant, pioneer and associate of Charles Annis) ran an inn
near Kingston Road from 1808. It was a popular stopping-place
and served as quarters for British soldiers during the War of 1812.
For the duration of the war, Roger Conant's entire wealth in gold

and silver lay behind a removable knot in a pine board and remained safe. The Annis family were staunch pillars of the Methodist church and held services regularly in their home. When Elizabeth, a daughter of Levi and Rhoda, married Anthony Washington, a local Methodist preacher, the Sunday evening scripture readings became a regular service. Neighbours frequently attended these services 'at Washingtons'.' In 1838 a church of logs was completed which was known as Washington Church. It was replaced in 1885 and the second building stood until 1960. The manse, built of brick (as was the church), is at 14 Centre Street and is still lived in today.

Jeremiah Annis was the eleventh son of Levi and Rhoda. His fieldstone house, with a well-proportioned verandah in front, was built in 1867. It is now a restaurant and has been much altered, but still stands on its original site on Kingston Road at Scarborough Golf Club Road just slightly east of the junction with Eglinton Avenue. Jeremiah was a versatile man who served as licensing com-

Marshall Macklin house, Brimley Road

missioner, Justice of the Peace, and township councillor. A Liberal in politics, he was a close friend of George Brown, founder of the Toronto *Globe.*

The Annis clan spread throughout Scarborough. In the 1840s, Andrew Annis built 'The Manor,' another fine example of fieldstone construction, at Port Union Road and Danforth's Trail (now called Colonel Danforth Trail). This house seems to have been a gathering place for the family. The property led down to Lake Ontario and on social occasions boating, fishing, and fox-hunting were enjoyed. This pleasant stone house which for so many years played an important part in community life was demolished in 1974 to be replaced by a brewers' warehouse outlet.

Although stone buildings predominate in Scarborough, there are also some interesting brick buildings to be seen. Among these is the house built in 1867 by John Perryman Wheler, mill owner. Wheler came to Canada from Devonshire at the age of 19. He operated a sawmill and flour mill powered by the water of Highland Creek, and built a Victorian Gothic brick house. Today the house is set behind the Bendale Bible Chapel on the west side of Bellamy Road south of Lawrence Avenue. It is a 'bank' house typical of the period, built so that the parlour and bedrooms were entered by a front door at ground level, while access to the large combined kitchen, dining-room, and living-room was from the rear of the house, also at ground level but on the lower part of the slope. This lower level opened directly to the work section at the rear, barns, sheds, etc. Like many other Scarborough men, John Wheler was a strong Reformer.

The Richardson house at 27 Old Kingston Road affords a pleasing contrast of old red brick with elaborate white mouldings of exceptional intricacy. The first storey was built in 1824 of wood and the second storey was added later when the wood was bricked over. The curved side windows and the fine tracery work are evidence of this later date. The verandah adds simple lines to complement the ornate gable. This house has been occupied by members of the Richardson family since it was built.

A group of early brick houses belonging to the L'Amoreaux family are located in the north-west corner of Scarborough. They were built for Josue L'Amoreaux (grandson of a French Huguenot, André L'Amoreaux), who spent some time in New Brunswick with other Loyalist Huguenot families before coming to Upper Canada. (The name has also been spelled L'Amoroux and L'Amareux, as noted previously.) The best L'Amoreaux houses are on Passmore Street, west of Kennedy Road. A recent fire destroyed the barns on this property but the original weathered board-and-batten house remains as well as a later brick building with all-over patterning in three colours of brick. Simpson Rennie, son of early Scottish settlers, bought the property in 1838. He made many improvements to the farm and in 1883 was awarded the Ontario Agricultural and Arts Association gold medal for the best managed farm in several counties. The first brick schoolhouse in Scarborough township was located on the L'Amoreaux property.

One member of the L'Amoreaux family, Jacob, was imprisoned after the Mackenzie Rebellion. He was only one of many in Scarborough on whom suspicion of disloyalty rested, as it was known the Reformers were supported by some of the most prominent families - the Kennedys, Annises, L'Amoreaux, and others.

Richardson house, 27 Old Kingston Road

James Kennedy, a United Empire Loyalist, came from Schenectady, New York, to Scarborough in 1800 and settled in the bush along what is now Kennedy Road. He returned to the United States in the 1830s but many of his family and descendants remained. A Kennedy house built in the 1850s is at 2756 Kennedy Road. The earlier part, dating from 1857, was built at the back of mud brick. The front, of patterned brick, is of a later date.

A fine brick house, also from the 1850s, located at 2656 Midland Avenue at the corner of Sheppard, was once the manse of the United Church. The original wooden church was built in 1848 and later replaced by a brick building. The house of patterned brick is in fine condition and surprises the onlooker in its location, surrounded as it is by mid-20th-century styles.

The Reesor family, one of the chief pioneer families in the county, came originally from Switzerland to the United States in the 1730s. They settled mainly in Markham and much of their history

Peter Reesor house, Steeles Avenue

is detailed in the chapter on that township. However, three Reesor houses are near to and on Steeles Avenue, close to Markham Township. The Simeon Reesor house, at the north end of Reesor Road, is of board and batten, and the date of construction, 1857, is carved into the house. Near by there remains evidence of a sawmill. Two white frame Reesor houses on Steeles Avenue, east of Reesor Road, are probably on what was the Peter Reesor farm; one was built in the 1860s and the other constructed later to replace buildings used by farmhands. Proximity to a mill probably accounts for the choice of wood as the building material. The houses incorporate the simple charm of what had become the classic indigenous architecture – the simple porch, the gable flanked by two chimneys, and the beautiful, symmetrical windows.

Land in Scarborough which was worth $5 an acre in 1815 was valued at $100,000 an acre in some areas in 1976. Development is constantly changing the contour of the present borough, and yet if one looks for it carefully, the striking beauty of the past is visible, juxtaposed with the present. The name recalls the time when Mrs John Graves Simcoe called the township after Scarborough, England, for upon sight of the famous Bluffs she was immediately reminded of that North Sea coast.

15

Etobicoke

The name 'Toby Cook,' which appears on several early maps, refers to the river and land area known after the early days of settlement as Etobicoke. 'Toby Cook' is, however, more probably a mispronunciation of an Indian word meaning 'the place where the alders grow,' than the name of some unknown adventurous pioneer.

What is certain is that settlement started at the beginning of the 19th century and began with the settling of discharged soldiers from Simcoe's Queen's Rangers, and of United Empire Loyalists. The lakefront was then a wilderness, and the land grants given were an invitation to years of clearing the bush for settlement and travelling over miserable roads. One of the largest grants was made to Colonel the Honourable Samuel Bois Smith, who owned 1530 acres stretching from the lake to what is now Bloor Street. Because of the military and government connections of those who settled in Etobicoke, the district was quite solidly behind the Family Compact during the Rebellion - William Lyon Mackenzie found little support there.

The Mimico area was called by the Indians, 'place of the wild pigeon.' The now extinct passenger pigeon flocked in the woods in millions at the time settlement began. The birds decimated the farmers' crops before harvest time and consequently they were destroyed by the settlers. In addition, the clearing of the forest areas removed their natural habitat, and eventually the species became extinct.

The clear waters of the Humber River and the proximity to market at York gave rise to an unusual number of thriving mills in the township. Although no house remains to recall William Gamble, first reeve of Etobicoke, the remains of one of his mills can be seen by the Old Mill Restaurant at 21 Old Mill Road. This mill links the names of its builder, William Tyrrell, and its owner, William Gamble, pioneer of Etobicoke. The remains today show five stories of the mill which burned in 1881, but the first mill on this site was constructed in 1793. It was built for the government by Nicholas Miller of New York State, of logs and boards. It was run for the government, leased to Thomas Fisher, and then sold by the government to Gamble in 1835. At the time of its construction, Etobicoke had been in government hands for only six years, having been purchased from the Indians in 1787 for £1700 in cash and merchandise. The early mill on this site was thus built before Etobicoke was surveyed, and before the disbanded militia and the United Empire Loyalists formed the first settlement near Lake Ontario and began to cut through the bush to clear the land. Mrs Simcoe, wife of the first

The old mill on the Humber

lieutenant-governor, recalled that period when she wrote in her diary of the killing of 700 rattlesnakes during construction.

After Gamble purchased the mill from the government in 1835, he erected a new five-storey mill on the site, using materials brought up the Humber River in barges. This mill burned down in 1847 and was replaced the following year by a new seven-storey mill, the remains of which we see today. William Tyrrell was the builder of both mills. He later became prominent in the area and was known as the 'Squire of Weston.' His imposing home, built in the 1850s, may still be seen today at 64 John Street in Weston. This house is also of interest because during the 1860s it was occupied by Trinity College School, now located in Port Hope, Ontario.

The Gamble family is recorded in the first crown grants in Etobicoke. John Gamble received land in 1802 and joined the disbanded Rangers and the Loyalists on the lake front. He was of a Scottish family, the eldest son of Dr John Gamble, and was, like his younger brother, a miller. It is unfortunate that the homes which John and William built no longer exist. The remains of William's mill are all that recall the man who was miller, merchant, postmaster, woollen manufacturer, and lumber merchant, and who produced such essentials as oatmeal, nails, and bone fertilizer, and who provided a dry kiln slaughterhouse, blacksmith shop, cooperage, wagon shop, and dwellings for his workers.

Scarlett Road recalls the name of John Scarlett, a wealthy pioneer, who came to Etobicoke with £60,000 sterling and began to buy up land. He built a sawmill, and owned flour mills and a distillery as well as a brickyard on Dundas Street. John Scarlett, like Gamble and other mill owners, gave work to many labourers in the area and brought prosperity and settlement to Etobicoke. By 1836, Scarlett had built a racetrack called 'Simcoe Chase,' a welcome diversion in those hard days.

John's son Edward inherited the sawmill and kept it until it was sold to Matthew Canning in 1871. Edward's imposing house is still standing, and is in excellent condition at 15 La Rush Drive. Built in 1848, it is typical of many of the finer homes of the period. It has a handsome front door and balanced, two-storey construction. The marble for the two fireplaces was imported from England. On the face of one the name 'Scarlett' has been scratched, possibly by a careless workman. It is thought that the front door was also brought from England.

Another Scarlett house, at 11 Yorkleigh Avenue, was owned by St George Scarlett, Edward's brother. It has been altered, but the basic structure is similar to that of the house on La Rush Drive. The wings and bay windows are clearly later additions, but the entrance is almost identical with that in Edward's home. The same side and top lighting surround a door with carved moulding only slightly different from that of the brother's. A third Scarlett brother was also a mill owner. He owned property to the south of Edward's. In all, this industrious family possessed three sawmills, a distillery, brickyards, a racecourse, and property on the Humber which included Lots 14 to 19 in Concession C and Lot 18 in Concession B.

North of the Scarlett holding was the Musson property, also located on the Humber River and consisting of Lots 27, 28, 29, and 32, Concession B. Thomas and Edward Musson owned a distillery and a sawmill here, but moved in 1840 to what is now Islington, where they bought land in the Clergy Block. They purchased their

Edward Scarlett house, 15 La Rush Drive

property from Truman Wilcox, and their home, 'Musson Place,' is at 4884 Dundas Street, Islington. This building served as a home, store, and post office. Alterations have been made to the front of the house where a door with curved mouldings is the central feature. The windows have been changed, but the back of the house is in its original state – as so often happens, the clue to the age of the house is the back, for when alterations or 'modernization' took place, it was always done in the front, and the back of the house was frequently left as it was, early windows and original glass panes often remaining in the rear. 'Musson Place' now houses an antique shop and is part of a crowded commercial area of Dundas Street. At an earlier time, it was set off by spacious grounds and was a gracious and attractive home.

The other Musson house, credited to Edward and built shortly after he moved down from the Humber, is located at 189 Burnhamthorpe Road, at Kipling Avenue. Here again, alterations have been

Edward Musson house, 189 Burnhamthorpe Road

made. The door is now enclosed by a small porch and a new room
has been added, but it remains a very attractive house. It is said that
at one time the Mussons held garden parties here, for the property
stretched to Mimico Creek and made a lovely setting for such affairs. When Edward owned this house he was a well-established citizen who contributed to community life. He was chosen as the first
township clerk when Etobicoke was established in 1850. He served
on the council and in 1858 was elected reeve. A descendant of the
Mussons was the founder of the Musson Publishing Company.

The life of a pioneer in Etobicoke is described by John Grubb of
Edinburgh in his letters written to Scotland from the time of his
arrival in Etobicoke in 1833. Grubb was a man of some wealth when
he emigrated to Upper Canada, and on his arrival he purchased property on a branch of the Humber, 150 acres on either side of what is
now the Albion Road. John and his son erected a log house immediately, but two years later, in 1835, John built 'Elm Bank,' which

'Elm Bank,' 19 Jason Road, Thistletown

still stands on the Humber. Today its address is 19 Jason Road, Thistletown. John Grubb had no experience in agriculture, having lived in the city of Edinburgh, but he was energetic and adaptable. No sooner had he built his log house than he began hauling stones from the Humber riverbed for 'Elm Bank.' The stone building standing a few feet away from the house was originally the servants' quarters and was at one time connected by both underground and aboveground passages. 'Elm Bank' is a particularly attractive and unusual home. It is now owned by a descendant of John Grubb.

John's son William had arrived in Etobicoke in the year before his father. According to the *History of the County of York*, he and an uncle who accompanied him had a hazardous voyage:

After a rough passage, extending over six weeks, they were ultimately wrecked on the coast of New Brunswick, losing their personal effects, but fortunately without loss of life. After a delay of six weeks, during which time they re-

Former servants' quarters for 'Elm Bank,' 23 Jason Road

mained without shelter, they were taken to Quebec and thence to Montreal, from which city they removed to Toronto after a stay there of ten days.

John's other son, Andrew, built another stone house, 'Braeburn,' near by, some time between 1835 and 1850. It was destroyed by fire in 1852 and rebuilt, using the same stone, in 1853. It has since been removed, stone by stone, and reconstructed in Black Creek Pioneer Village.

John Grubb was a campaigner for better roads. He describes (quoted in *The York Pioneer*, Centennial Edition, 1969) the hazards of travel, which in the winter depended on enough snow for sleighs and at other times was vulnerable to the ravages of storms:

The breaking up of the river was like the winter, very wrathy and wicked. You can tell your good uncle that within the memory of the oldest inhabitant it never raged and bellowed so before. On Sunday morning the 14th of March, the ice bridges and trees came down the West Branch like an avalanche carrying the very farm before it. Through the flats it came, warning the old Plank Road Bridge to keep out of the way. But the old bridge gave for answer that she had stood the ice and floods for the last 20 years and she was going to show pluck in her old age and wouldn't stir for all the water in the branch. But, alas, in her boasting she forgot her rotting carcass. She stood the shock bravely but the pressure was too great from behind and with a groan and a yell she bade farewell forever to the West Branch. Our little barn bridge saved herself all but a few scratches by some sleight of hand.

You will wonder how the travellers got over the river, dangerous when the water was high, the current was very strong at the brewery. After delay, the men of Vaughan had to come down in a body and make the river on both sides passable, and in consequence have got all the praise which they certainly deserve.

By 1840, John Grubb had cultivated 120 acres of his farm property by the Humber and was raising horses, cattle, and sheep. He was elected councillor of Etobicoke in 1842:

Our elections for Home District Councillors put me at the head of the poll by a great majority over all grades of politicians.

He was now in a position to press for better roads. One of his letters to Edinburgh describes the countryside and the state of the roads:

To compare a small thing with a great, while riding along the road the other day toward the beautiful, picturesque and may I add, romantic village of Weston where the bank of the Humber is seen in nature's wildest grace. There the busy mills and tanyards are concealed in the glens below, while the decent church crowns the neighbouring heights, all indicating the appearance of health and happiness ...

For many years the road to this place has been, like all other statute labour roads, in a wretched state owing to the great travel carried on from the many flour and saw mills to Toronto, with the addition of much farm produce from the fertile soil along the banks of the river, from the Gore and Albion townships.

As president of the Weston Road Company and later the Albion Plank Road Company, Grubb saw plank toll roads which were passable in all weather built right up to the villages of King Township, and to Toronto.

Montgomery's Inn, Dundas Street

Dundas was a main route leading out of York and Thomas Montgomery's inn was operating in Etobicoke in 1833 to offer its amenities to the local residents or to travellers. Still located at Dundas Street and Montgomery Road, this old inn is Loyalist Georgian at its best, and shows the results of recent authentic and tasteful restoration by the Etobicoke Historical Society. It is open daily to the public for a small admission fee.

The innkeeper, Thomas Montgomery, came to Etobicoke from Ireland in 1812, and began by operating an inn in a temporary structure. His success as innkeeper led to his building first a frame tavern and then, in 1832, the present fieldstone inn. The building has interesting architectural features. The windows have sidelights and are almost square in proportion. The building, a sizeable one for its early date, has strong horizontal lines in the roof which accentuate its length. The wily Montgomery encouraged local farmers to take advantage of his hospitality by cutting a road through his

4681 Dundas Street West

property to the Old Mill so that they passed by his tavern on their way to and from the mill. This path is now called Montgomery Road.

The inn was typical in that it served as the hub of settlement business before town halls or public meeting-places were built. Montgomery's Inn held in its upper ballroom public meetings of every sort from auction sales to council gatherings – the first council of Etobicoke met there from 1846 to 1849. This ballroom also served the needs of local carousers and sometimes provided a dormitory for them after the ball. On other occasions the ballroom was used as a magistrate's court. Montgomery's Inn had two basement rooms which were used for the temporary confinement of suspected wrongdoers and the nickname, 'Bridge of Sighs,' was given to the stairs which linked them to the ballroom 'court.'

At 4681 Dundas Street West is a fine Georgian house once owned by Tom Montgomery's son William. Built in the 1830s, it was greatly enlarged in 1850 and purchased by William Montgomery in 1870.

36 Rathburn Road, Thorncrest Village, home of a
Father of Confederation

This building is set back from the road and the clean Georgian lines are displayed in a well-treed setting behind a picket fence.

In Thorncrest Village, at 36 Rathburn Road, is the home of Sir William Pearce Howland, a Father of Confederation and lieutenant-governor of Ontario from 1868 to 1873. Howland's board-and-batten house is set on a fieldstone foundation. The original frame has been covered with new siding. A wing was added in 1890 and the front windows changed, but the back windows and door are of an early date. This building was the Howlands' summer home, which stood on their farmland.

William Howland had established his family in the milling industry in 1840. Today, when the river flow has diminished, it is remarkable to learn that in the early 1800s the Humber River supported the mills of Howland, Gamble, Scarlett, and Musson. In 1845, William Howland built a flour mill five storeys high on the Humber.

John Moore house, 18 Great Oak Drive

Typical of the many small storey-and-a-half farmhouses in York County is the compact and attractive home at 18 Great Oak Drive, built for John Moore. The bricks used in its construction were made on the property. Houses with a full second storey were then taxed at a much higher rate and therefore many owners, like Moore, chose to forgo the convenience of a full second floor in view of the substantial saving. This house is said to possess a ghost, but a benevolent one. The present owners affirm that the smell of freshly baked bread is sometimes evident at an early hour of the morning. This inviting odour lasts for only a few minutes and then disappears. The Moore house has been tastefully and authentically restored.

Two houses represent the Coulter family in Etobicoke; they are credited to Robert Coulter of County Down, Ireland, who came to Canada in 1822. 'Elmbrook Farms' is a large imposing Georgian home located at 515 Etobicoke Drive. It was built of brick, but is

'Elmbrook Farms,' 515 Etobicoke Drive

now covered with frame. The assessment rolls of the township confirm that the house was standing on this site in 1854, so it was
probably built by Robert Coulter for his bride, Ann Jane Patterson,
some time between their marriage in 1851 and that date. Coulter
must have had a prosperous career to be able at age 31 to start construction on this large scale; it would have been more usual for a
young couple to live in a smaller dwelling for several years. The
brick for the Coulter house was made on the property. Robert
Coulter was a farmer, but the addition of pillars and portico to the
front of the house in later years indicates a degree of affluence
which came from supplementing farming with the breeding of
horses and with a lumber business. The second Coulter house is at
112 Ravencrest Drive. It also predates 1855 and is a smaller brick
building; it is possible the Coulters lived first in this location on the
Humber while the larger house was being built. They raised twelve

'Applewood,' 471 Burnhamthorpe Road, birthplace of
J.S. Woodsworth

children and the *History of the County of York* records in 1885 that no death had occurred on the Coulter farm for 50 years - a remarkable feat in those days of high infant mortality.

Andrew Bigham was one of the first settlers in Etobicoke, receiving his crown grant in 1802. The house which is now located at the corner of Rathburn and Martingrove roads was built by his son, Samuel Woods Bigham, but probably was preceded by earlier buildings of Andrew's own on this property. When Andrew Bigham came to his grant of land, he would have done as so many others and constructed a shanty of logs or a log cabin, but he must soon have made plans for the larger stone house we see today. The house was on this site in 1854, and could have been there as early as 1844. By the time it was built the Bigham family had neighbours, but when Samuel's father Andrew first settled on his holdings, Etobicoke was so sparsely populated that he had no neighbours for four years. In spite of this Andrew did not lack company for he married twice and had seven children by his first wife and nine by the second.

Of historical and political interest is a neat brick house at 471 Burnhamthorpe Road, just west of Highway 27. Known as 'Applewood,' it was the birthplace of James Shaver Woodsworth, the founder of the CCF, now the NDP. The house was built in 1832 by Peter Shaver, and it is now owned and occupied by a descendant.

The spire of St George's-on-the-Hill has been a landmark on Dundas Street since 1847 when it was built to house a pioneer congregation which had been meeting in a log schoolhouse. Rev. Walter Stennett, who left the principalship of Upper Canada College for Roche's Point and built Christ Church Roche's Point in 1862, was one of the weekly ministers. The first permanent rector of St George's was 'that colourful pioneer cleric, Doctor Thomas Philipps.' In the words of Henry Scadding, Philipps was 'a divine, well-read, - a perfect Vicar of Wakefield type, and one of the last gentlemen to powder his hair.' The land for the church was the gift of William Gamble, who, along with Thomas Fisher and Edward Musson, paid the difference when the inevitable problem of costs exceeding estimates arose. The structure was 'of rough-cast with the old-fashioned large windows, but the most striking feature was the lofty spire rising above the trees in height a hundred feet, whose tinned sides sparkled and gleamed in the sunlight so as to be visible for miles around.' Rev. Mr H.C. Cooper, who became rector in 1849, painted the watercolour of the church which is inside the door today.

St George's-on-the-Hill, Dundas Street

SELECTED BIBLIOGRAPHY

ABRAHAMSON, UNA. *God Bless Our Home*. Toronto, 1966

ADAM, G. MERCER and REV. HENRY SCADDING. *Toronto Old and New*. Toronto, 1891

ANDRÉ, JOHN. *William Berczy*. Toronto, 1967

ARTHUR, ERIC. *Toronto, No Mean City*. Toronto, 1964

BLAKE, VERSCHOYLE BENSON and RALPH GREENHILL. *Rural Ontario*. Toronto, 1969

BONIS, ROBERT. *A History of Scarborough*. Scarborough, 1965

BROWN, J.J. *Ideas in Exile*. Toronto, 1967

CARELESS, J.M.S. *The Pioneers*. Toronto, 1968

COUSINS, NORMAN. *In God We Trust*. New York, 1958

CREIGHTON, LUELLA. *The Elegant Canadians*. Toronto, 1967

DAVIES, BLODWEN. *A String of Amber*. Vancouver, 1973

DUNHAM, MABEL. *The Trail of the Conestoga*. Toronto, 1942

FIRTH, EDITH G., ed. *The Town of York 1793-1815*. Toronto, 1961

FITZGERALD, DORIS M. *Thornhill: An Ontario Village*. Thornhill, 1964

GIBBON, JOHN MURRAY. *The Romance of the Canadian Canoe*. Toronto, 1951

GILLHAM, ELIZABETH McCLURE. *Early Settlements of King Township, Ontario*. King City, 1975

GIVEN, ROBERT A. *The Story of Etobicoke*. Etobicoke, 1973

GLAZEBROOK, G.P. deT. *Life in Ontario*. Toronto, 1968

GUILLET, EDWIN C. *The Pioneer Farmer and Backwoodsman*, Vols. 1 and 2. Toronto, 1964

- *Pioneer Arts and Crafts*. Toronto, 1968
- *Pioneer Life in the County of York*. Toronto, 1946
- *Early Life in Upper Canada*. Toronto, 1933
HANNAY, JAMES D.C.L. *History of the War of 1812*. Toronto, 1905
HART, PATRICIA W. *Pioneering in North York*. Toronto, 1968
HETT, FRANCIS PAGET. *Georgina*. Toronto, 1939
Historical Sketch of Markham Township. Markham, 1950
History of the County of York. 2 vols. Toronto, 1885
History of the Town of Newmarket. Newmarket, n.d.
HOLBROOK, STEWART H. *Dreamers of the American Dream*. Garden City, 1957
Illustrated Historical Atlas of the County of York. Toronto, 1878
JAMESON, ANNA BROWNELL. *Winter Studies and Summer Rambles in Canada*. London, 1838
JUKES, MARY. *New Life in Old Houses*. Toronto, 1966
KILBOURN, WILLIAM. *Religion in Canada: the Spiritual Development of a Nation*. Toronto, 1968
LANGTON, H.H., ed. *A Gentlewoman in Upper Canada*. Toronto, 1950
LANGTON, W.A., ed. *Early Days in Upper Canada: Letters of John Langton*. Toronto, 1926
MACRAE, MARION and ANTHONY ADAMSON. *The Ancestral Roof*. Toronto, 1963
MIDDLETON, JESSIE EDGAR. *The Municipality of Toronto, a History*. 3 vols. Toronto, 1923
MIERS, EARL SCHENCK, ed. *The American Story*. New York, 1956
MILLER, AUDREY SAUNDERS, ed. *The Journals of Mary O'Brien 1828-1838*. Toronto, 1968
MINHINNICK, JEANNE. *At Home in Upper Canada*. Toronto, 1970
MITCHELL, JOHN. *The Settlement of York County*. Toronto, 1952
MOODIE, SUSANNAH. *Roughing It in the Bush*. 2 vols. London, 1852
MURRAY, FLORENCE B., ed. *Muskoka and Haliburton 1615-1875*. Toronto, 1963
NEWMAN, LENA. *An Historical Almanac of Canada*. Toronto, 1967
PRATT, E.V. *A General Etymological Historical Examination of the Place Names of York County*. Guelph, 1970
REAMAN, G. ELMORE. *A History of Vaughan Township*. Toronto, 1971
REMPEL, JOHN I. *Building with Wood*. Toronto, 1967
ROBERTSON, JOHN ROSS. *Landmarks of Toronto*. 6 vols. Toronto, 1894-1914

- , ed. *The Diary of Mrs. John Graves Simcoe*. Toronto, 1911

ROLLING, GLADYS M. *East Gwillimbury in the Nineteenth Century*. Toronto, 1971

ROSE, GEORGE MACLEAN. *A Cyclopaedia of Canadian Biography*. Toronto, 1886

SCADDING, REV. HENRY. *Toronto of Old*. Toronto, 1873

- and JOHN CHARLES DENT. *Toronto, Past and Present: Historical and Descriptive*. Toronto, 1884

TALMAN, JAMES J. *Basic Documents in Canadian History*. Toronto, 1959

VAN STEEN, MARCUS. *Governor Simcoe and His Lady*. Toronto, 1969

YORK PIONEER AND HISTORICAL SOCIETY. *Annual Reports*.

INDEX